The Old Villages
of Denbighshire
and Flintshire

Dewi Roberts

GWASG Carreg Gwalch

ISBN: 0-86381-562-6

Cover photos: St David's Church, Pantasaph;
Bodelwyddan Church;
Dyserth from above the falls.

Cover design: Alan Jones

First published in 1999 by Gwasg Carreg Gwalch,
12 Iard yr Orsaf, Llanrwst, Wales LL26 0EH
☎ (01492) 642031
Printed and published in Wales.

The author

Dewi Roberts lives in a Denbighshire village, and this is his eighth book. His other works include *Visitors Delight, A Clwyd Anthology, The Land of Old Renown, Christmas in Wales, Both Sides of the Border* and *An Anglesey Anthology*. He is a member of the *Academi* and is active as a reviewer and speaker on literary and historical topics. He is now at work on a further book.

Contents

The Old Villages of Denbighshire and Flintshire

Wales is a land of villages and small rural communities have played a significant role in the history of the nation. In this informative book Dewi Roberts guides us knowledgeably around thirty five small communities in North East Wales and focuses on many of their historical facets, some of them unexpected. We discover, for example, that Dyserth was the scene of industrial riots in the nineteenth century, that Nantglyn has a yew tree which incorporates a pulpit, read an eyewitness account of a wartime air disaster at Llanfair D.C. and learn of the remarkable Ffoulke Owen and the circumstances surrounding his death.

Anecdotage and folklore will also be found here, and the book will prove an ideal handbook to take with you as you travel around the two counties. The accompanying photographs aptly compliment the text.

When advance extracts from Dewi Roberts' book appeared in our newspaper we had some very encouraging feedback and the series was a great success. Mr Roberts is a lively and entertaining writer and his book deserves to be a great popular success.

Neil Gibson: *Denbighshire Free Press*

Introduction

Wales is a land of villages, and small rural communities have played a significant role in the shaping of the history of the nation. Not only have numerous significant historical events taken place within their boundaries, but they have also produced men and women who have contributed to the life and culture of Wales.

This book is intended as a very modest introduction to certain facets of the history of selected villages in both Denbighshire and Flintshire. I have used the old county boundaries to enable me to include some villages which were in the pre-1974 Denbighshire, but which have now been exiled by the powers-that-be to the new county of Conwy; villages such as Pentrefoelas, Llansannan and Llannefydd, none of which I wanted to exclude from this book.

Some of the villages covered here were the birthplace of men and women who have devoted much of their lives to the study of every aspect of the history of their respective parishes, and have preserved their painstaking research in the form of books, pamphlets and articles. I have drawn upon their writings in these pages, and wish to express my indebtedness to them.

The items on Denbighshire originally appeared in the form of a series of articles in the *Denbighshire Free Press* and I am grateful to the newspaper for commissioning them, and also for providing many of the photographs reproduced here. My particular thanks to Neil Gibson and Mari Catrin Jones and to photographers Katja Diedrick, Neville Pratt and Tony Humphreys. I myself took the photographs in the Flintshire villages.

The staff of the Denbighshire Archives Department at Ruthin were, as always, most helpful and I also wish to warmly thank Carol Shone, the community librarian at Buckley, and Tristan Grey Hulse, who is always capable of shedding new light on the most abstruse areas of history research.

Finally a word of thanks to my publisher, Myrddin ap Dafydd, for his enthusiastic response when I suggested the idea of this publication to him, and also to my wife, Pamela, for driving me along the highways and byways of the two counties in my quest for information.

Dewi Roberts,
Llanrhaeadr,
Vale of Clwyd.

The 'Marble Church', Bodelwyddan

Denbighshire

Bodelwyddan

Bodelwyddan is situated just off the busy A55 between St Asaph and Abergele. The name translates as 'the abode of Elwyddan'. Elwyddan was the brother of Cyndrwyn, a prince of ancient Powys, who is thought to have lived in this part of Denbighshire for a time.

The steeple of St Margaret's Church, popularly known as 'The Marble Church', rises to a height of over 200 feet and is a prominent landmark in the flat surrounding landscape.

One visitor wrote of this steeple in caustic terms. He observed in a travel book that it reminded him of:

'. . . a certain kind of wire brush which I use for cleaning my gun.'

He must have had his tongue firmly in his cheek for, by general agreement, the steeple, and indeed the church in general, is in the finest tradition of nineteenth century ecclesiastical architecture. One cannot help but admire the very precise and exacting work involved in the creation of many of the fine features. The wooden lectern alone is reckoned to be the result of six thousand hours of work, and is one of the finest examples of its kind from the last century. There are a hundred and thirty carved portraits in stone, both within the church and outside, and these offer an enduring reminder of the dedicated skills of the carvers involved. It is called 'The Marble Church' on account of the many kinds of decorative marble used for the floor and pillars.

The Bodelwyddan estate became the seat of Sir William Williams (1634-1700), who became Speaker of the House of Commons. His elder son, William, became a forebear of the Williams-Wynn family of Wynnstay, the most notable of all the gentry families in North Wales.

The Williams family rebuilt what had been an earlier structure. In the nineteenth century one of the family decided that the new building should be Gothic and castellated in style. The work was undertaken over a number of years, and the resulting building was a mock castle similar to Gwrych Castle near Abergele. Work on the architectural features was supervised by a man named Hansom, whose name is most commonly associated with the Hansom cab. He was also responsible for the design of St Beuno's College near Tremeirchion.

In 1829 another member of the family, Margaret Williams, married

Henry Peto, the sixteenth Baron Willoughby de Broke of Warwickshire. When he died in 1852, she returned to Bodelwyddan. Because of her love of the area she wished to see the creation of Bodelwyddan as a parish in its own right, separate from that of St Asaph. The then Bishop of St Asaph complied with this plan and Lady Margaret's brother, Hugh, who had succeeded to the baronetcy in 1858, was also enthusiastic in his support. The church was the most important part of this entire enterprise, and the Williams' commissioned John Gibson, a distinguished figure in his field, to work on the design. It was Lady Margaret's intention from the outset that, apart from anything else, the church should be a memorial to her late husband. It was consecrated in August 1860.

In 1915 Bodelwyddan Castle and the estate were requisitioned for military purposes. A number of hospital buildings were erected and these were an extension of the large Kinmel Park transit camp nearby. When the army left in 1920 the building was converted into Lowther College, a girls boarding school, which established a high reputation. Its success over the years was largely due to the enthusiasm of the first head, Miss Lindley. The school closed in 1982, partly as the result of growing financial pressures.

The building was eventually purchased by Clwyd County Council, as it was then, for £500,000.

Today the Castle has much to offer the visitor. It houses an invaluable collection of paintings from the National Portrait Gallery in London, while the accommodation part of the building now constitutes the largest hotel in North Wales. It is surrounded by the most delightful woodlands and gardens.

The Kinmel Estate has also played a significant role in the history of the area. Edward Hughes purchased the estate in 1786. His wife inherited some derelict land in Anglesey. When copper was discovered on this uninviting area, Hughes was quick to realise the potential and invested a good deal of money to enable it to be extracted. Parys Mountain became an important source for the supply of copper, and he was well able to afford a new manor on the Kinmel estate.

His wealth was enhanced still further during the period of the hostilities with France, when the demand for food grew. On the estate was marshland extending as far as Y Foryd at Rhyl. Hughes was able to drain this land in order to make it fertile and suitable for the grazing of stock.

Kinmel has provided employment for countless local people over many generations. In the nineteenth century, following the death of another member of the Hughes family, the estate was split up and several farms and cottages were sold.

19,000 troops, several of them Canadian, were billeted at Kinmel Army Camp during the first world war. At the end of the war, one of the most disturbing incidents in the history of north-eastern Wales during the twentieth century occurred at the camp. The war-weary Canadians, who had survived the worst extremities of warfare in the French trenches, wanted nothing more than to be repatriated. But their promised passage home was delayed again and again. They lived in squalid and overcrowded conditions, and when influenza struck some of them wasted away. Those who did survive still did not have any sailing dates honoured, and rumours began to circulate that they would not be going home, the army having other plans for them.

In March 1919 the situation became explosive and the men squabbled among themselves, and this eventually accelerated into violence and bloodshed. They ran amok, setting fire to huts and looting. They were fired upon by their own countrymen, and there were five deaths from gunshot wounds.

Ever since, there has been a reluctance by the authorities to discuss these events, but some years ago a Canadian production company joined forces with the BBC to produce a feature film based on these terrible incidents. It was called *Going Home*, and both Canadian and Welsh actors took part.

In the churchyard at Bodelwyddan are the graves of the Canadians who died. On one of these is the poignant inscription:

'Some day, some time, we will understand.'

St Stephen's Church, Bodfari

Bodfari

Bodfari is situated four miles from Denbigh on the A541 Mold road.

A Roman outpost was probably situated near the junction of the rivers Clwyd and Wheeler, near here. Various artefacts have been discovered in this area which lend support to this, such as the discovery of urns, and fragments of weapons.

There is a great deal of speculation about the route of a Roman road which ran through the area, close to the village, and ended at Deva (Chester).

To the east is Moel y Gaer, a Celtic fortification. It would have offered a vantage point from which to protect the pass which we now refer to as 'the Bodfari gap'. One nineteenth century historian suggested that a great battle between Boadicea and the Romans took place there. This seems extremely unlikely, as there is some doubt as to whether the Queen of the Britons ever set foot in this part of Wales.

On the east side of the road which leads up to the central part of the village is an old tap, which ceased to supply water many years ago. One is unlikely to be able to find the tap unless one is actually searching for it carefully. There now seems to be little doubt about the fact that this was the site of a holy well of some importance. This means that, contrary to common assumption, Bodfari had two such sites, and not one. The other is higher up the hill, adjoining the churchyard, and was incorporated within the premises of the Dinorben Arms when the inn was being extended several years ago.

There can be no doubt that both wells have fulfilled important needs but there has been a tendency, due to limited knowledge, to confuse the reputation and history of the nowadays more obscure well with the much publicised one at the Dinorben. The Dinorben well is certainly very ancient, and could date from Roman times, but unfortunately any real knowledge of it is limited.

As for the well known as Ffynnon Ddier, named after St Dier – and there are a number of variants on the spelling of this name – its origins were described in the twelfth century by Robert of Shrewsbury.

'This man indeed, for his Sanctity in those days, and miraculous testimonies thereof, famously renowned; for by his prayers he had raised out of the ground a goodly spring in a place that was dry before.'

He then goes on to refer to the fact that the water had:

' . . . a supernatural force to cure all sores and diseases of such as did drink thereof, or wash their sores therewith.'

This well assumed a particular reputation for permanently soothing babies who cried habitually in the night. Following a visit in 1699 Edward Llwyd wrote:

'It is the custom for the poorest person in the parish to offer chickens after going nine times round the well. A cockerel for a boy and a pullet for a girl. The child is dipped up to his neck at three corners of the well. This is to prevent their crying at night.'

A more recent reference to the well occurs in the Report of the Royal Commissioners of 1912.

'On the left of a footpath leading from the main road towards the railway, about 180 yards from Bodfari church, is a neglected and choked spring, the surroundings of which answer to Edward Llwyd's description.'

The church was dedicated twice, firstly to St Dier and later to St Stephen, after whom the present church derives its name. It is thought that he could have been buried close to the original church. This would have been built of wattle, with an earthen floor covered with rushes. There would have been a plain stone altar.

A church register dating back to the sixteenth century contains an entry of marriages. It also has other items within its pages, such as a reference to the purchase of *The Holy Bible in the Welsh Tongue* in 1592. There is also evidence of exceptionally severe winters between 1605 and 1608, and of beggars dying of starvation.

There is a tale concerning two thieves who stole horses which they discovered tied to a tree outside the church. On discovering their loss, the owners entered the church and placed unlit candles on the altar. The spirit of St Dier must have been very much in evidence it seems, and he made his presence known to the men by lighting the candles as they knelt praying for the return of their valuable horses. As a result, the thieves were unable to make any progress in their attempt to get away from the village and, as in a bad dream, the further they tried to gallop the more immobile they became. The horses eventually brought them back to the churchyard where they were discovered by the rightful owners. The horses were grazing in the grass, but the thieves stood absolutely motionless with stupefied expressions on their faces.

This is one of the rich repository of folklore stories which can bring a fascinating element into local history research.

But now we move on to the nineteenth century.

An occasion to remember took place at Bodfari on September 2nd 1869, when the village celebrated the opening of the railway line between Denbigh and Mold. The driving force behind the initiative, it seems, was Captain Pennant of Brynbella, Tremeirchion. Shortly before noon, crowds flocked to the station platform to await the arrival of a special train which was due to arrive from Denbigh. As the magnificent engine drew into Bodfari, there were cheers from the crowd and the children waved the Union Jack. More cheering took place as the immaculately dressed passengers alighted. They included Captain Pennant and his party, a detachment of the Denbighshire Yeomanry Cavalry, the Mayors and respective Corporations of Denbigh and Ruthin, the Bodfari Old Fellow's Lodge, and members of the Bodfari Benefit Club. An address was delivered by Captain Pennant, and there were even louder cheers and a chorus of 'For he's a jolly good fellow'. Later there was a tea party in a field adjoining the station. But that was not all, for in the evening there was a celebratory dinner in the village schoolroom, the food being provided by the Dinorben Arms.

The famous liberal reformer and publisher Thomas Gee (1815-1898) owned an iron mine close to the village for a time. Carts containing haematite would be loaded at the mine, and taken down to the railway station. From here they would be conveyed to Foryd Harbour in Rhyl, where the cargo would be put on board ships bound for France. There is little information available about the mine, and we do not know when Gee took it over. But it seems that following his death, his family sold it. He was a familiar figure in Bodfari at that time, for he would ride from his home in Denbigh on his horse 'Degwm' to inspect his mine, and would also sometimes visit the village in order to deliver a sermon on Sundays.

Ffynnon Fair (St Mary's Well), *Cefn Meiriadog*

Cefn Meiriadog

The village of Cefn Meiriadog is five miles from St Asaph.

The community, which is situated in a well wooded part of the Elwy Valley, takes its name from Saint Meiriadog. He was a monk at a Celtic monastery, and probably had a cell on the banks of Afon Elwy. His brother Mael was also a monk and when they both decided to leave North Wales, Meiriadog moved to Cornwall. Later he moved to Brittany, and there attempted to propagate his faith. He became particularly associated with Pluvigner in southern Brittany, although during his final years he lived near Pontivy, in the middle part of the country. It was here that he died in approximately 575. He is still a much respected saint in Brittany, and pilgrims still visit the chapel and holy well which Meiriadog created in Pluvigner.

With this historical and spiritual connection in common, the people of Pluvigner and Cefn Meiriadog are anxious to perpetuate the memory of the saint. This resulted in members of Cefn Meiriadog Historical Society, myself included, spending a week in Pluvigner three years ago, when we were given an extremely warm welcome by local people. During that visit we went to a number of significant Celtic holy sites in the southern part of the country.

The historical society was established in 1977 and, with a consistently faithful membership, it meets each month in order to participate in excursions, arrange a series of winter lectures, and involve itself in local projects.

Some time ago, for example, they became involved in the maintenance of Ffynnon Fair (*St Mary's Well*), which is situated on private land below Wigfair Hall. This ruined site has provided a focus for research by historians for many years, although some questions still remain unanswered. But we do know that there was once a bridge over the Elwy which was once part of a well worn route used by travellers, pilgrims included, between Denbigh, Wigfair and Henllan. Peter Roberts, a public notary of the late sixteenth century, kept a journal in which he recorded life in the area at that time, and at one point he refers to the destruction of the 'Chappel Bridge' following heavy flooding in the Elwy Valley in October 1624. Roberts also refers to the fact that clandestine marriages took place on the site. Presumably, these would be conducted after sunset, when it was illegal for marriages to take place. However, if rewarded with an incentive, a willing vicar choral from the cathedral at St Asaph would often agree to take the service.

The well had long been thought to contain water with curative powers, but during his reign Henry VIII suppressed the monasteries and other holy sites, including holy wells. As a result Ffynnon Fair was consigned to neglect.

In about 1840 the well was fenced off from the surrounding meadowland, and a 'picturesque' garden created on the site. Today little remains of this, although the ruinous structure of the building gives us a clear impression of what it must have looked like at an earlier period.

Following a visit to Ffynnon Fair and the surrounding area, the great English poet Gerard Manley Hopkins wrote his well known poem *In the Valley of the Elwy*.

The area has achieved international status in terms of its archaeological interest because of the evidence of Stone Age life which has been unearthed there.

Pontnewydd Cave stands on a slope, high on the side of the Elwy valley. Our forebears lived at the mouth of this important cave some 230,000 years ago. They would have been hunters and gatherers, and able to spot wild animals as they moved through the wooded area in the valley below. They were dependent for their existence on the hunting and killing of these animals, and the remains of bison, reindeer, ox and deer have been found on the site. A major excavation was conducted by Dr Stephen Green and his team from Liverpool University in the nineteen seventies.

During the last war the cave was sealed off by the army, and a doorway was inserted with a brick surround. It was used as an arms storage centre.

Wigfair Hall, mentioned earlier, is a fairly recent building, but an older dwelling once stood on the same site. This became the home of the bard Siôn Tudur (1522-1602), who was much admired for his literary qualities. Several years of his life were spent outside Wales, however, in the service of both Prince Edward and Queen Elizabeth.

Plas-yn-Cefn is one of the homes of the most prominent North Wales gentry family, the Williams-Wynn's. Work on this impressive mansion began in 1597, and various improvements were made in subsequent centuries. St Mary's Church was consecrated in 1865, as a memorial to the premature death of one of the family.

A fairly short distance from Plas-yn-Cefn is Dolben, which was built by a retired sea captain in the eighteenth century, and acquired by the Williams-Wynn's in 1832.

I will end with a lighthearted anecdote from more recent times. About eighty years ago a fair was being held at St Asaph, the main focus of interest being a crocodile. Unfortunately it died suddenly, and was bourne away from the fairground by two young men, presumably to be buried. However, under cover of darkness, they transported the body to the caves at Cefn Meiriadog, in the hope that they might throw the world of archaeology into complete confusion! They spent the following day telling everyone they met about an amazing discovery which they had made! This resulted in national newspaper interest. However the hoax was eventually discovered, and a lenient police office ordered the two men concerned to carry the heavy, and by now rather smelly, crocodile corpse back to St Asaph, where they had to bury it.

Dyserth Waterfall

Dyserth

Invaders came into Denbighshire across the coastal plain of north-east Wales, and defences were necessary to guard the route. One of these was at Dyserth, and a settlement evolved around this defence.

Situated on the slopes of Moel Hiraddug, Dyserth is some three and a half miles from Rhyl. The main focus of interest nowadays for visitors is the waterfall, which is formed from a stream from St Asaph's Well (*Ffynnon Asaph*) in the adjoining parish of Cwm. During his travels through North Wales in 1774, Dr Samuel Johnson visited the upper reaches of the fall with Mrs Thrale. He tells us that he 'trudged unwillingly' behind his friend, and was 'not sorry to find it dry'.

Lower Dyserth is the older part of the community, and is referred to in the Domesday Book as Dissard.

Dyserth Castle has had a chequered history. It was built by Henry III in 1241, and remained in his hands for several years until Llywelyn ap Gruffudd waged a fierce battle, and destroyed it in 1263. In this skirmish a notable chieftain, Einion, the son of Rhirid Flaidd was killed. A cross was erected in his memory, and the shaft is said to have been used at a later date to form a stile into the churchyard. The ground on which a National School was built in the last century was named Bryn Einion, in order to commemorate the ancient leader.

A nineteenth century writer tells us that:

' . . . the fragments of the castle show that its ruin was not effected by time; they lie in vast masses, overthrown by mining, which was a common method of besieging, long before the use of gunpowder.'

There was once a ruin in a field of a building called Siambr Wen, and this is reputed to have been the home of Sir Robert Pounderling, who was once the constable of the castle. He apparently had one of his eyes gouged out by a Welshman in a tournament. When years later he was asked whether he would like to have a further test of armed skill arranged with the same Welshman, he declined, saying that he had no intention of giving the man the opportunity to remove his other eye!

The church, which was substantially rebuilt in the nineteenth century, is dedicated to St Cwyfan. Parts of the building date from the thirteenth and fourteenth centuries. Certain notable marriages have taken place here, including that between Thomas Mostyn and the widow of Bishop Parry. There is an early fifteenth century tomb stone.

Dyserth figures in the history of witchcraft in North Wales. In the seventeenth century Henry John James was engaged in this activity, and apart from casting a spell on humans, he was also able to afflict animals through his powers. One day he discovered a hog in his garden, and the spell which James cast on it made it very ill. It did recover eventually however. On another occasion he bewitched a man named Randle Peers, whom he had developed a dislike towards. Peers too became seriously ill, and died.

People like James were certainly not the exception in village communities in the past, and the notorious Llanddona witches of Ynys Môn spring immediately to mind.

Close to the site of what was the castle were the Talargoch mines, which according to one account:

'... produced more lead ore than any other mine in the country in the eighteenth century.'

They had been worked since the Roman occupation of Britain, and in the seventeenth century one of the earliest Joint Stock Companies in Wales was established, with a view to mining there.

The Talargoch Lead Mines were situated on the boundary between the parishes of Dyserth and Meliden. It was leased to the London Mining Company in 1699, and by the mid-nineteenth century yielded £2,000 in annual profits, which was no mean sum at that time. It gave employment to around a hundred men.

There were obvious health hazards involved in mining at the time. The men worked at a considerable depth, and breathed in ore dust every working day.

In July 1856, due to a combination of grievances, the men went on strike. Their main concern arose from the fact that the employers wished to introduce new working regulations. The men made it clear that they were fully prepared to arbitrate with the employers under the mediation of the local magistrates. But any move towards resolving matters peacefully was destroyed by an outbreak of violence.

Some twenty-five men, no doubt inspired by the Rebecca rioters and dressed in women's clothing, surrounded Dyserth Hall, the home of Ishmael Jones, an agent for the company, and brandished firearms which they fired before riding into the night. But this was by no means the end of the matter, for on a subsequent night a number of men met and proceeded in the direction of the mine. They again fired shots, but this time a watchman was injured. A reward of £200 was offered for information about the incident.

The magistrates decided to bring in soldiers from Chester, and thirty-five troops were posted at Talargoch for a week. However, there was no opposition from the miners, and before the soldiers returned to Chester the strikers had agreed to return to work. The affect on them was counter-productive, for forty of them were dismissed.

To the west of the village, on the Rhuddlan road, is Bodrhyddan Hall, parts of which date from the late seventeenth century. Historically this has been the seat of the Conwy family, and the present owners are Lord and Lady Langford. There is some very fine parkland, and a focal feature is Ffynnon Fair (*St Mary's Well*), not particularly ancient but thought to have been designed by Inigo Jones in 1612. There was something of a passion for the picaresque in the landscape design of the period, and it was not uncommon to find such features within the grounds of fine houses.

Dyserth today is a fairly peaceful village, with extensive views down to the coast in one direction, and towards the Vale of Clwyd in the other. But only a few miles away is the tourist razzmatazz of Rhyl, a town which came into being within much more recent times.

The bridge over the Dee at Carrog.

Glyndyfrdwy and Carrog

Glyndyfrdwy, literally translated 'the valley of the Dee', is situated on the A5 between Llangollen and Corwen.

The entire region of Edeirnion, in which both these villages lie, is inextricably associated with the most famous leader in Welsh history: Owain Glyndŵr.

He was born Owain ap Gruffudd Fychan on the family estate at Glyndyfrdwy in 1359, and took the name by which we know him from Glyndyfrdwy. On the estate there was much game to be hunted, and the nearness of the Dee ensured that the dining table frequently offered trout and salmon. The family were very comfortably off, and had an even more prestigious home at Sycharth, in the border country not far from Oswestry.

When he was ten Owain's father died, and his son inherited the estates. He decided upon a career in law and undertook the necessary studies in London. It was during this period that he had a dispute about property with a neighbour, Lord Grey of Rhuthun. Glyndŵr went through the official channels in an attempt to get a decision which would favour his strong claim to the property. When Siôn Trefor, the Bishop of St Asaph petitioned the English parliament on his behalf, the response was dismissive in the extreme:

'What care we for these barefoot rascals.'

Glyndŵr was enraged and soon gathered sympathisers around him. On a fair day in 1400 he attacked Rhuthun, and soon afterwards, supporters from every part of Wales allied themselves to his fight against injustice.

The conflict at Rhuthun ignited a fuse which spread from the north-east, and was destined to shape the course of Welsh history. Soon, Glyndŵr had bases at Aberystwyth and Harlech. He maintained his war against Henry IV for fifteen years, and was notable not only as a man of action, but also as a statesman. Parliaments were held at Pennal and Machynlleth, and Glyndŵr was elevated to a status which no other Welshman had achieved.

In 1406, however, the English crown was reasserting itself and Owain Glyndŵr began to lose his grasp on power. Despite this, people in the uplands of Wales still supported him, and it was not until 1413 that his cause finally seemed doomed. The information which we have about him after that is fragmentary, unreliable, and often derived from folklore rather than from historical fact. 'Some say that at the end he came like a dog to lie in Glyndyfrdwy among the scenes of his youth,' writes H.V. Morton.

According to a traditional prophecy Glyndŵr is not, in fact, dead at all but merely sleeping and awaiting a call to rise again, should Wales ever have need of his services. It is hardly surprising that he remains a potent symbol of nationalism for the Welsh people.

Glyndyfrdwy's neighbouring village, Llansantffraid, is now more commonly known as Carrog. The change of name was introduced with the coming of the railway, during the last century. This brought an ever-increasing number of middle-class English visitors to the area. The railway authorities therefore decided that Llansantffraid was beyond the powers of pronunciation of many tourists, and so changed it to Carrog. This name was selected in an entirely arbitrary way because there happened to be a farm of the same name in the area. At that time, as now, it was a favourite place for anglers. Coracles were a commonplace sight on the Dee at that time.

A feature, which makes Carrog a little unusual among villages of a similar size, is the long row of Victorian and early Edwardian houses, which were built mainly by wealthy people from Merseyside. They served as holiday homes, and sprang up following the inroads which the Great Western Railway Company made in revolutionising travel over distances in rural Wales.

There was once a house known as 'Carchardy Owain', in which Glyndŵr is reputed to have imprisoned opponents. Whether the building, which no longer exists, was ever used for that purpose is open to doubt.

Close to the Dee, which is spanned by a magnificent bridge dated 1661, is the tumulus known as the Mount of Glyndŵr. When George Borrow travelled through Edeirnion in 1854 he was told by a local:

'This is the hill of Glyndŵr where he was in the habit of standing to look out for enemies coming from Chester.'

However it seems more likely that it was erected before Glyndŵr's time, and that an ancient people could have buried their leader there. This is certainly the view which Borrow himself favoured.

The original church which served the community was dedicated to Ffraid, a sixth century saint. It seems possible that the remains of the church survived until 1601. In that year, the last remnants of the ruin were swept away by very severe flooding. *The Archaeologia Cambrensis* of 1893 carried a paper headed 'Interesting Discovery at Carrog'. It revealed how in May of that year the water of the Dee was exceptionally low. A local farmer and his men were removing stones from the bed of the river for building purposes when they discovered a solid oak beam. Soon afterwards, a further six beams came to light. There were indentations in them which strongly suggested that they could have come from a church.

The fact that the final ruins of the church were finally carried away by the flood is recorded in the traditional lines:

The Dee of the great leaps
Took Llansantffraid church,
The sacred books
And the silver chalice also.

The Sunday School began in an upper room of the 'Grouse Inn', which is rather ironic considering the strong temperance ideals of the non-conformists.

Quarrying and farm labouring were the main sources of employment, and in 1900 no less than 199 men worked at Penarth and Moel Fferna quarries. Today Carrog is a popular stopping off point for tourists who take the steam railway excursions from Llangollen, which are proving so popular.

Writing in 1898 A.G. Bradley relates how the old men in the Glyndyfrdwy and Carrog areas still used to talk of Owain Glyndŵr as if he were still alive. One realises how vastly rural Wales and its people have changed in the last hundred and fifty years. The unrecorded past can be lost in a single generation.

Llindir Inn, Henllan

Henllan

Situated on the B5382, this village is often thought of nowadays as a suburb of Denbigh, which is only two and a half miles away. It has a feature which has aroused both curiosity and speculation for many years, for the main body of the church is quite separate from its tower, which is situated on a rocky prominence in the north-east corner of the churchyard. Theories have been put forward as to why this should be so. One of these maintains that the original church was destroyed by fire, and the new church built away from the tower which had escaped the inferno. But a more likely reason is connected with the extensive size of the original parish. This was sixteen miles long and seven miles wide, and it was felt that by situating the tower on the rocky outcrop, the bell would be heard over a wider area.

The parish was named after St Sadwrn, who is thought to have administered sacraments here in the sixth century. His work is documented by Robert, the Prior of Shrewsbury. It is thought that St Winifred passed through Henllan while making her way from Holywell to Gwytherin, where she remained until her death.

During the eighteenth century, a number of landed gentry families dominated the social life of the area. They administered the life of the village, and provided employment for working people. No less than forty people were employed on one estate within the same period.

The pews in the church were clearly allocated to the 'top families', and when this custom was ignored, it was quite common for legal action to follow. Anyone who challenged the upper classes had to face the consequences. But, to their credit, the gentry played a prominent, if not very successful, role in the education of the children of the parish. The eighteenth century Charity and Circulating schools offered inadequate learning, and what the children were taught was restricted to what their superiors thought they should learn in order to keep them well within their own social sphere. Little had changed in the nineteenth century. In 1847 attainment was reported to be poor, and this was hardly surprising. An Irish master was attempting to teach English to boys who were Welsh. Schooling took place in inadequate buildings, where there was little day light or fresh air.

The one and only public house in the village is the Llindir Inn, which is a thatched thirteenth century building, and one of the oldest buildings of its kind in Wales. Up to some forty five years ago, prior to a complete refurbishment, it retained its rough and ready nineteenth century tavern atmosphere. The inn has been much publicised over the years because of its ghost. Some visitors to the inn claim to have seen an attractive woman in white. It is not known when she and her quick tempered sea-faring husband kept the inn, but it appears that while he was away, the lady craved male company. She took a virile lover, but unfortunately for them, her husband found himself on unexpected shore leave and returned home late one winter night. When he discovered the couple in a compromising position, he murdered his wife. From that time onwards her spirit has refused to rest. Ghost stories abound, but this one held public attention. In the sixties a number of investigators stayed at the inn in an attempt to obtain a sighting of the lady concerned. Among these was the then television reporter on the 'Tonight' programme, Macdonald Hastings. An elderly barman related how he had encountered the ghost, and had told her in unequivocally Anglo-Saxon terms where to go!

Another tale concerning the inn involves a conjuror. He visited the inn in the early nineteenth century, and ordered bread and wine. But he felt that the charge for this refreshment was too high. Instead of disputing the bill he decided on a more effective way of dealing with the situation. He slipped a piece of folded paper under the leg of a table in the bar, and went on his way. When a maid came to collect the plate, her feet suddenly began to dance as rapidly as her legs would allow. She burst into song:

Six and four are ten, count it o'er again,
Six and four are ten, count it o'er again.

When the landlord saw what was happening he bawled at her to stop, but to no avail. He moved forward with the intention of knocking some sense into her, when he too was caught up in the dancing hysteria. By now the landlord's wife had heard the commotion. She yelled at them to stop, but no sooner were the words out of her mouth than she fell into the grip of the conjuror's spell. A village boy was sent at full speed to catch up with the conjuror on the Llansannan road, and he eventually returned with instructions to remove a piece of paper which he would find under a table leg. This done, the crazy, involuntary dancing stopped as abruptly as it had begun, and one is left wondering whether any subsequent guests were overcharged?

Two important figures who were born near Henllan were Humphrey Llwyd and Robert Parry. Humphrey Llwyd was born at Foxhall, which is less than a mile from the village. He was a considerable scholar and is remembered today mainly for his work in the field of cartography. He prepared the first maps of Wales and published a number of books.

Robert Parry was born in Tywysog in 1540 and is now remembered chiefly because of the fascinating diary which he kept, which is a mine of information about the events of his lifetime. He fought against the Spanish Armada and wrote a novel called *Moderatus*.

Within the last thirty-five years Henllan has changed considerably. In the smaller village of the nineteen fifties, there was a branch of the Welsh chain grocers E.B. Jones, a further general grocery shop called Evans and Jones', a smaller grocery shop in Llindir Street, a butcher's shop, a greengrocer's and a part-time barber's shop. Now there is just the combined post office and shop, and many village people do the bulk of their shopping at the Denbigh supermarkets. Older natives of the village tend to refer to the 'new people', as they describe them, who have moved there within the last twenty years. This reminds me of the slightly caustic lines penned by a villager in the nineteenth century:

Henllan church and Henllan steeple
Are the emblem of Henllan people,
All at variance, what's the wonder
When church and steeple are asunder.

St Garmon's Church

Llanarmon-yn-Iâl

Llanarmon-yn-Iâl is situated between Corwen and Hawarden near the A494. Iâl is the Welsh for a hilly area, and the name was adopted by a local family as their surname, the best known member of that family being Elihu Yale, the benefactor of Yale University.

Some significant archaeological finds have been made in the area. In the nineteenth century a cave was discovered which contained the bones of a number of animals, including the brown bear.

St Garmon's Church could originally have been founded when Germanus, a Celtic saint, visited the area bringing his own message of Christian faith. The original church was probably a crude construction of daub and wattle, or perhaps even just an outdoor assembly point with a cross.

If you visit the present church look out for one of its most interesting features, an effigy of a thirteenth century crusader.

Like many other parishes in North Wales, Llanarmon was administered by clerics who had no real interest in the church, or the people. They lived outside the area, reaping the financial rewards of their positions. This was much resented by many parishioners, and eventually an act was passed which made it obligatory for vicars to live in rectories within their parishes, and to play a far greater role in the spiritual life of the community.

In the nineteenth century the church owned a great deal of land in the countryside, and farmers, as often as not, rented church land. The level of tithe payments was set in the eighteen thirties. It was in the eighteen eighties, however, that things started to go very badly wrong. During that decade there were a series of poor harvests, with the result that farmers could no longer afford to pay the amounts involved. In any case, they were non-conformists and would not tolerate their hard earned and inadequate income going to support the Anglican Church, with which they had no truck. As a result the church authorities seized farmers goods, including livestock. Auctions would be held to collect the money due, and as a result there were violent scenes. Eviction, selling-up and destitution often followed, and some of the families ended up in parish workhouses. The writer E. Tegla Davies based his novel, *Gŵr Pen y Bryn* against the background of these riots as they affected Llanarmon.

Leadmining in the area began in earnest in the middle of the eighteenth century. In their heyday, two of the mines employed hundreds of men. Many of the employees combined mining with farming, a hard life indeed. Eventually mines were no longer workable because of the amount of extraction that had already taken place.

A little more than a hundred years ago, many skilled trades were practised in Llanarmon including the milling of corn, butchering, and wheel-making. There was also a blacksmith, a baker, a milliner and a tailor.

Prior to the coming of the motor car the parish was, of necessity, self contained. Now villagers drive to the supermarkets at Wrexham or Mold in order to replenish their supplies.

A general view of Llanbedr

Llanbedr Dyffryn Clwyd

Llanbedr is situated on the A494 Rhuthun-Mold road, and is in a delightful position in the shadow of the Clwydian Hills. The wealth of early historical events which have occurred in these hills is well documented, but it is worth including an account here of something that occurred during a more recent period. In February 1773 there was an exceptionally strong storm which put the inhabitants of Llanbedr, and other neighbouring villages, in fear of their lives. It was described in the Annual Register for that year:

> 'The night before last Moel Fama was heard to utter groans and the hills trembled to their roots. The noise was like the sound of thunder from the rolling of huge stones which were rolling down the hills. In an hour there was a loud clapp and the vortex of the hills threw up in the same instant vast bodies of combustible matter; all nature seemed to make a grand effort and rent one side of the mountain, which was of solid stone, into a haiatus . . . The summit of the hill tumbled into this vast opening . . . '

The present church is Victorian, but the ruins of the old parish church (Old St Peter's), are situated on a hill above the village within close proximity to Llanbedr Hall. Certain pews in the church are recorded as having been rented. A plan reveals that the congregation would sit in pews which clearly reflected their place in the social hierarchy, the landed gentry occupying the pews nearest the front. Possibly the notion was that by doing so they were nearer to God, but it was more likely to have been activated by an acute feeling of social superiority. At the very back a reservation was marked 'Common', and one can only guess what kind of person might have worshipped there!

For some years the churchyards of Old St Peter's and the present church were being used simultaneously, and the first person to be interred in the present one died in 1865.

For many years the owners of Llanbedr Hall arranged for the care of both the new church and its churchyard. The responsibility was taken over by the Parish Council in 1920. The church was consecrated by the Bishop of the Diocese in 1864, the foundation stone having been laid by Sarah Margaret Jesse in 1863. Her father, John Jesse of Llanbedr Hall, was a surgeon and a man of some repute locally.

Prior to Jesse's ownership, the Hall was lived in by Joseph Ablett. He was an important figure in the Vale of Clwyd in the nineteenth century. His philanthropic work included the donation of many acres of land at

Denbigh to enable the North Wales Lunatic Asylum to be built. He was also a Member of Parliament for an English constituency, and a patron of the arts. In this capacity he became friendly with some of the literary luminaries of his day, and some of these visited Llanbedr. The poet and essayist Leigh Hunt recalled his visit with great affection:

'To come into the Vale of Clwyd is to realise the dreams of books . . . Ablett's is a very fine house, with very fine grounds, situated in a most beautiful country like a garden, with the gentle Welsh mountains framing the picture all round.'

Another well known writer of the period was Walter Savage Landor and he refers to the fact that Ablett erected his own tombstone in order to

' . . . induce other people to overcome their prejudices against this situation.'

There were strict house rules for servants who were employed at the Hall. These were inscribed in slate in the servants' hall, and underneath is the date 1829.

The speaking of Welsh was prohibited, and anyone caught speaking in his or her native tongue was fined a penny. Even more serious was taking the Lord's name in vain, for which the offender had to pay what was in those days the heavy fine of six pence; for cursing, swearing or telling lies, threepence would be extracted from the wages.

In 1930 Llanbedr Hall became a private sanatorium for the treatment of tuberculosis, which was so widespread at that time. This was due to the immense initiative of Hugh Morriston Davies, who gained renown within his specialised field of medicine. The Hall ceased to be a sanatorium in the early fifties.

The toll-gate, the revenue of which was invested in the Turnpike Trust for the benefit of the parish poor, was taken off its hinges in May 1875 and placed against the church wall. The toll-gate was sited at the Gate Cottage on the Rhuthun to Mold road. The building is still standing.

A house called Tan-y-bwlch acted as a school for a time until a purpose-built school was established in 1874. This was a National School, and was sited on freehold land donated by John Jesse.

John Puleston Jones was born in Llanbedr in 1862 and was blinded in an accident at an early age. Despite his lack of sight, he pursued an education at the universities of Glasgow and Oxford. He became an ordained Calvinistic Methodist minister in 1888 and made a name for himself as a theologian and essayist. He pioneered a Braille system in the Welsh language which is still in use.

Llanbedr retains much of its old-world charm. In a poem written shortly after a visit to Llanbedr, Leigh Hunt wrote:

'Quitting dear friends with homeward care
In the sweet land that held the Druid,
I touch'd at thee, Llanbedr fair,
Thou lily of the Vale of Clwyd.

Gardens I saw, home's fringes bright, –
A homestead Church, and pastoral valleys
And mountains green of gentle might,
Luring ascent with leafy alleys.

A page from out a Poet's book
It was, – choice Nature's adorning. –
A landscape worth an angel's look, –
A landscape of God on Eden's morning.'

Llannefydd: a general view

The 'Hawk and Buckle', Llannefydd

40

Llannefydd (Conwy)

If you visit Llannefydd today the impression is one of complete rural calm, and you might find it difficult to imagine a time when it was the scene of some of the most severe rioting in Wales.

This erupted in 1888 when resentful farmers in the area made a valiant stand against the church tithes, or taxes. The church had the power to demand that farm produce and stock be seized from farmers, who could ill afford the amounts which they were forced to pay. Eight bailiffs and thirty police officers, led by an official named Stephens, set out from Denbigh for Llannefydd, but when they arrived at the village, they were faced by a formidable crowd of a thousand angry protesters. They jeered the officials, and stones began to hurtle through the air. When an attempt was made to calm troubled waters, things became even worse. Blows were struck and the situation was really ugly.

When the officials arrived at a certain farm, a large section of the crowd surrounded them in an intimidating way. One man beat a drum in Stephens' ears, and he retaliated by attacking the man. This ignited a further fuse of violence, and free fighting quickly broke out. The bailiffs and police produced truncheons, which they used without any consideration of the injuries they were inflicting. According to a contemporary newspaper report:

'they cracked the craniums of those nearest at hand and had no regard for age or size. Their victims included children under fifteen, men over seventy, and women.'

Dr Pritchard was summoned from Denbigh to attend to their wounds. The Chief Constable read the Riot Act, but despite this, determined attempts were made to renew the attack. When the officials eventually returned to Denbigh, they were greeted by threats of further violence from some of the townspeople, and, but for the intervention of the mayor, there would have been further bloodshed.

A local heroine of the riots was Ellen Jones of Nant Ucha, who became known as 'The Queen of Llannefydd'.

This was not the first time that Llannefydd had been the scene of violent unrest, for by the final decade of the eighteenth century the price of bread rose to an unacceptable level. It was the staple diet and many families were unable to afford it, and suffered deprivation. This hunger situation led to some unpleasant scenes. A crowd of four hundred stormed Abergele armed with home made weapons, and attacked a man whom they knew had tried to persuade other men not to participate in militancy. Miners from Flintshire roamed from village to village in their desperate search for grain. Soldiers were sent to Llannefydd following disturbances, and some thirty men were sent for trial on law and order offences. A farm labourer had been shot dead.

But the history of the village was by no means always a fiery one. For most of its long history it has been a fairly typical Welsh upland community, dependent for its livelihood on what it could produce from the land. The weather was a key factor of course, and a poor harvest could have serious consequences.

The parish population increased considerably in the eighteenth century, and there is evidence of some people living to a ripe old age.

It was commonplace in rural areas for children to work, and some were employed to scare birds while other picked stones.

Knitting was a cottage industry in which both men and women participated. The resulting items were sold at local fairs, of which there were four in Llannefydd each year.

As in other villages many different trades were carried out, including that of gun making. The man who carried out this work in Llannefydd was something of a 'character', and local boys would climb on to the low roof of his cottage and clog his chimney up with mud and stones. This resulted in his kitchen, being consumed in smoke and in a fit of temper, and much to their delight, he would rush out and chase them.

Another village character was, it seems, a man of dubious morals. He was once asked by Thomas Gee, 'What kind of a heart does a sinner have?' to which he replied, 'It is cold and as hard as a rock.'

There were some small copper mines in the area, offering modest deposits. They were generally only worked in winter, when there was a reduction in the amount of work which needed doing on the land.

There are references to the mining of coal between 1832 and 1895. When it was optimistically assumed that there might be large deposits, there was serious discussion about the possible construction of a railway line to Llannefydd for its transport. The idea was that it would leave the Vale of Clwyd Line at a point close to Trefnant and run parallel to Afon Elwy, and then branch off to a suitable transportation point.

It was discussed over a long period but eventually it was not considered feasible. One of the problems would have been that of obtaining the consent of local landowners for the line to run through their property.

During the eighteenth century the village was on the main stage coach route to Ireland.

In 1903 post was delivered to Llannefydd by pony and trap from

Trefnant, and at that time there were three public houses there, The Cross Keys, The Kings' Head and the one which remains today, the Hawk and Buckle.

It would be difficult today to find a village which is more peaceful than Llannefydd, but we should not forget its importance in the rural history of north-eastern Wales and the violence, resulting from injustice, which took place there.

Tegla's Well, Llandegla

Llandegla

Llandegla is situated to the west of the Llandegla moors; that wide, bleak open tract of countryside between the Vale of Clwyd and Wrexham.

The church is dedicated to Tegla whom, according to tradition, was converted to Christianity by the Apostle Paul and martyred by Nero. A notable feature within the building is a fifteenth century chandelier, which is a considerable rarity. Coincidentally, you will find another one in St Garmon's Church in the neighbouring village of Llanarmon-yn-Iâl.

In the nineteenth century the church was restored considerably, partly due to a generous donation from Lady Willoughby de Broke of Bodelwyddan.

Near the church is a healing well which is reputed to be the second oldest in Britain. In the past, it was a famous resort for those seeking a cure for epilepsy, or the 'falling sickness' as it was known. A rather bizarre ritual had to be performed in order to enable the sufferer to derive beneficial results. Firstly he would have to wash his limbs in the well, and then drop four pennies into the water. Afterwards, he would walk around the well three times, reciting the Lord's Prayer each time. This was never performed until after sunset, and if the afflicted person was a man he would offer a cock to Tegla, and if a woman, a hen. The fowl would be carried in a basket, first around the churchyard, and then around the outside of the church. Then the bird would be taken inside the church, and the epileptic would lie down under the communion table with a Bible under his head. Covered with a carpet he would remain there until dawn, and would then donate a further six pennies to Tegla, leaving the fowl in the church. If the bird died it was assumed that the cure had been achieved, the disease having been transferred to the dead bird.

There are a number of tales of the supernatural associated with the area. Outside the village, on the Rhydtalog road, there have been some spectral sightings in the past. A number of travellers reported seeing a deeply frightening figure looming up in front of them on dark nights. Many years ago, by chance rather than design, a human skeleton was unearthed in a field at the side of the road and removed. From that time onwards there were no further supernatural occurrences there.

Writing in the sixteenth century the scholar and diarist Robert Parry refers to the fact that nine people, simultaneously, saw about three thousand armed men on horseback carrying banners:

' . . . whereas indeed there was no such thing but some apparition or forewarning of likelihood.'

A spirit once haunted the old rectory, making the life of the occupants miserable. It assumed a different guise each night. A local man named Griffiths had established something of a reputation as a ghostbuster, and he was called in to deal with this troublesome creature. One evening the spirit came in the form of a bluebottle fly, which Griffiths managed to trap in a small box. He then placed this under a stone in Afon Alun, beneath Llandegla mill bridge. Griffiths told the spirit that it would have to remain there until a tree grew and attained a certain height. But other villagers knew of this and were not as patient. According to Elias Owen, the North Wales antiquarian, they were in the habit of lopping the branches off the tree when it did eventually begin to grow. This fantastic story has it that the spirit still languishes in the same spot.

Llandegla figures in the history of the drovers in North Wales. A two mile stretch of the old highway which was once used by these colourful characters can still be traced to the east of the village. It was used as an overnight stop on the journey from Anglesey to the market in London. The animals would be allowed to graze in the fields while the drovers refreshed themselves at the inn and enjoyed a night's slumber. They would often ensure that their stock had access to the healing waters of the well, in the belief that this would guarantee their safe arrival in London.

Close to the village is what is commonly regarded as the finest Welsh earthwork. Tomen y Rhodwydd was once the site of a motte and bailey castle which was built by Owen Gwynedd in about 1149. It was attacked and burnt by Iorwerth Goch ap Maredudd of Powys, although it seems that it was restored during the reign of King John. It would effectively have guarded the nearby Nant-y-Garth Pass from enemy attack.

Bodidris Hall is situated a mile from the village. It derives its name from Llywelyn Aurdorchog, an ancient lord of Yale. When Thomas Pennant visited the house in the late eighteenth century he observed that it stood:

'. . . in two counties, Denbighshire and Flintshire; the long table in the hall having an end in each.'

Llandegla did not remain unaffected by the tithe disturbances of the eighteen eighties, for there was a good deal of violence both here and at Llanarmon. However in its intensity it does not really compare with the extreme conflict which occurred at Llannefydd. The strife involved was reflected in the writing of Edward Tegla Davies, who was born in Llandegla in 1880. He became one of the leading Welsh-language writers of this century. By profession he was a minister of religion, and in this calling he spent some years at Denbigh.

46

Llandyrnog

Situated to the east of Denbigh, Llandyrnog is protected on one side by the lofty Clwydian hills. On these hills many centuries ago a chain of posts were established, from which the approach of enemy forces could be clearly spotted. In cases of imminent danger the families of the area retreated with their flocks.

It is difficult nowadays to imagine such dangerous times, for as you stand in the middle of Llandyrnog gazing at the hills, all is peaceful. In 1886 the antiquary William Davis observed:

'A more beautiful situation than this parish affords can scarcely be found in the rich Vale of Clwyd.'

Time has not changed the appeal of the village and its environs.

The church is dedicated to Tyrnog, and is mentioned in 1254 in the Norwich Taxation documents. It is by now a predominantly fifteenth century building, characterised by a local perpendicular style. Restoration work took place in the late nineteenth century. The work was supervised by William Nestfield, who was a reputable church architect of his time. He supplied the font, pulpit, lectern and stalls. One of the most interesting features is the east window, with its depiction of the Crucification. The blood streaming from Christ's side and feet have been caught vividly in the stained glass.

Evidence suggests that the shape of the churchyard was once circular, which could indicate that what developed as a holy site could once have been the location of a pagan shrine. You will find a sundial in the grounds of the church inscribed 1746.

The memory of two local worthies are perpetuated. One is John Ashpool, of Plas Ashpool, who died in 1722 when he was only thirty. In the vestry is a portrait of William Roberts, a one time rector who became the Bishop of Bangor. He was buried in the chancel in 1665.

William Davis refers to the erection of a National School in 1840, and by 1856, there are known to have been a hundred and twenty children being educated there.

Glan-y-wern Hall is situated in rolling countryside, a mile or so from the village. It was built in 1780 and in the nineteenth century Colonel Humberton, one of the benefactors of the church, lived there.

For four years, from 1896 until 1900 it was an annex of the North Wales Lunatic Asylum.

During the second world war it became a military hospital, and it would be difficult to imagine a more appropriate place for the victims of

Glan-y-wern Hall, Llandyrnog

The fine east window of St Tyrnog's Church, Llandyrnog.

battle to recover, with its green parkland and ancient oaks.

The Cocoa Rooms, which are now used for a variety of social activities, were so named because they are a legacy of the Victorian temperance movement. These centres were opened in many villages throughout the country at the end of the last century, and provided non-alcoholic beverages, notably cocoa, for those who either had no wish to frequent the pubs, or had been 'converted'. Here village folk could exchange gossip, play draughts and read the newspapers of the day.

The creamery remains the largest employer in the village, and it opened in 1921. Prior to that, cheese was made at Green Farm.

Some years ago a WEA class began to study the history of the village, and this created the stimulus for those involved to form a village history group. They have already made a detailed survey of the churchyard inscriptions, and are currently in the process of compiling a booklet in which they will bring all their research together.

The community council also administers nearby Llangwyfan.

General view of Llanfair Dyffryn Clwyd

Llanfair Dyffryn Clwyd

Llanfair Dyffryn Clwyd is situated two miles from Rhuthun on the Wrexham road. There is a great deal of interesting, often curious, historical information about both the church and the community.

St Cynfarch and St Mary's church was built of wood and plaster, the floor consisting of flattened earth. It is thought that it was rebuilt in stone at the beginning of the fifteenth century, the original church having been destroyed by Owain Glyndŵr.

In the second half of the nineteenth century, the great age of church restoration, changes were made to give the building the fine appearance which we see today.

It is not known exactly how long burials have taken place in the churchyard, but it is possible that these may date as far back as the thirteenth century. Griffith Parry, who died in 1792, had this inscribed on his grave at his own request:

'Praises on tombs are trifles vainly spent,
A man's good life is his best monument.'

There were many other interesting inscriptions, but in the early nineteen sixties graves were removed and broken up, and the ground levelled. No record was kept. This caused some controversy at the time, and in a letter to *The Denbighshire Free Press* a local historian wrote:

'The old churchyard contained many old tombstones, each one a paragraph of local history.'

There was a time when the parish clerk would walk ahead of a funeral procession, tolling a small hand-bell. This was partly because of the narrowness of local lanes at that time.

On a more light-hearted note, there is a well authenticated anecdote concerning the church. Many years ago a much respected cleric agreed to take a harvest thanksgiving service. He arrived early and retired to the WC, which was situated close to the church. While there, he lit his pipe and threw the match down the seat. The service got under way and the cleric was on the point of announcing the first hymn when everyone became aware of the smell of burning. When the verger went outside to investigate, he discovered that the toilet was engulfed in flames.

In the eighteenth century, and contrary to Christian thinking, the church was dominated by status and class. Following a service the cleric would be the first to leave. When he reached the door, the rest of the congregation followed in order of social rank. Firstly there would be members of landed gentry families, and they would be followed by the respectable middle-class and tenant farmers. Finally, at the bottom of the hierarchy, there would be working class people, notably farm labourers. Acrimony would sometimes arise when two squires, who regarded themselves as social equals, vied with each other for the forward position.

The church was not above prescribing its own punishment on moral grounds. In his book *The Old Stone Crosses of the Vale of Clwyd* Elias Owen relates how these unfortunates would be expected to stand in the church during services, covered with a white sheet. This custom was commonplace until 1810.

Close to the War Memorial stand a row of former almshouses known as the Elizabeth Owen Houses. They were taken over by the Knights of St John ten years ago.

Of the fine mansions in the area, Ty Mawr should be mentioned. It was the home of Llywelyn Adams, a clerk of the peace in Denbighshire.

Sir John Henry Puleston was born at Plas Newydd in 1829. He became the Member of Parliament for Davenport and leading member of the Tory party of his day. He was also Constable of Caernarfon Castle.

In 1631 the village stocks were erected near the White Horse Inn; it was known as a 'Repentance Seat'. A variety of misdemeanours were punished here. There was also a whipping post where vagrants, those without work and fixed abode, would be thrashed.

In the middle of the nineteenth century the postal delivery was in the hands of Edward Jones of Rhuthun who would deliver a bundle of letters and leave them at the White Horse. These would be placed in a window, with the names of the recipient facing outwards so that the envelopes could be read from the street. Each day a crowd would gather outside in order to find out whether anything had arrived for them.

A very popular festival was Gŵyl Mabsant (Patron Saint's Festival) celebrated in September. It was an occasion of great jollity. 'Wakes' would be held which would continue for a week, and work was, where possible, abandoned. Elaborate preparations would be made beforehand and farmers kept 'open house' for their friends. Boxing, donkey racing and other sports would be held. The tradition was observed up to the early nineteenth century.

During the same period the cruel 'sport' of cockfighting was commonplace throughout Wales, and Llanfair Dyffryn Clwyd was no exception. It was not until 1849 that an Act of Parliament made this activity illegal.

At its height, the population of the parish was 1,227, but by 1911 this had declined to 900. This was due to the introduction of mechanisation in agriculture, which drastically reduced the amount of labour required; scythes and sickles were a thing of the past for many.

During the period of the Napoleonic wars the population was reduced for a different reason. Uniformed soldiers arrived in the parish with the objective of compelling every able-bodied man to enlist in their ranks; all protest was in vain.

There is also an account of an incident which occurred during the Second World War. A Lockheed Hudson transport plane, with a crew of thirteen on board, was flying over the area when it was struck by lightning. The pilot lost control of the plane, and it plunged down engulfed in flames and crashed close to a farm. All the men on board perished. Although the Lockheed Hudson was American built, it was being flown by an RAF squadron, the 24th. This occurred on 17th July 1942 and an eyewitness related his memories of that day to me:

'On the day in question I was out on my bicycle with my lifelong friend Mr R.J. Jones (Jack). We were in the vicinity of Llanfair and the day was fine and clear when we heard a plane. Then we saw it and we could clearly see the descending trajectory which could only mean one thing – it had to crash, and crash it did! There was utter carnage, and it would not be proper of me to detail the scene. One of the occupants had made an effort to bale out but the plane was too low and his parachute failed to open. He landed in the lane and was still alive when we arrived, but died in our presence. We helped to cover him with the parachute. The plane itself fell in the field alongside the lane, and was burning with such ferocity no one could get near it, but it was obvious that there were no survivors.

The fields nearby were used by Barn Stormers during the nineteen-thirties, when for a few bob you could have a bird's eye view of the village.

In my opinion, on that fateful day God gave Llanfair a few split seconds of his precious time. If he hadn't, Llanfair would have predated Lockerbie by forty years, and that is why the crash is important in the history of the village. It was later rumoured that the plane had come from Northern Ireland and had been sabotaged by the IRA. This is not so silly as it sounds, for the IRA had been active in Britain in the nineteen thirties and gave succour to our enemies throughout the war.'

The accident was also witnessed by the vicar at that time, the Reverend Williams, and on the following Sunday he held a special service, his text being from St John V, verse 13: 'Greater love hath no man than this, that a man lay down his life for his friends.'

A few months later the vicar's only son, who was a wireless operator/air gunner, was accidentally killed on an airfield, aged twenty one.

Llangwyfan Church

Llangwyfan

Situated to the east of Denbigh, the small community of Llangwyfan is set in some of the most beautiful countryside in North Wales. The church is dedicated to St Cwyfan.

As with so many other North Wales villages, the church is thought to be located on, or near to, the site of a very much earlier site of worship. In the process of the restoration work carried out there recently, workmen quite by chance revealed evidence of what could well be the earthen floor of a previous building. During the work, the building equipment being used caused considerable vibrations, and at one point this resulted in pieces of the plaster on the walls being dislodged. Underneath were discovered what were recognised as parts of murals. However, the limited funds available has meant that it has not been possible to remove all the plaster in order to carry out the highly specialised work which the restoration of church murals demand. It can only be hoped that one day the finance may be available with which to enable this work to be carried out.

The church registers go back to 1723 and, together with the other surrounding parishes, it was transferred from the diocese of Bangor to that of St Asaph in 1859. Archdeacon D.R. Thomas in his *History of the Diocese of St Asaph* tells us that the parish of Llangwyfan did not exceed 1,073 acres at the end of the nineteenth century, when his book was published. He goes on to tell us that it was mainly enclosed by the parish of Llandyrnog, with the remaining perimeter bordering on Pontbedw, which existed in its own right at that time.

In the churchyard lies the body of Foulk Jones whose life spans no less than three centuries. On his grave are the dates 1699-1801. Outside the church you will see the replica of the stocks. The original stocks were removed many years ago, and in their day they were used for the punishment of a variety of misdemeanours. The church was re-dedicated last year by the Archbishop of Wales.

The mansion of Fron Yw, now a retirement home, was the seat of the Madocks family. They claimed their descent from a High Sheriff of Denbighshire who married Jane Williams, the heiress of Fron Yw in 1664. Their great-great grandson, William Alexander Madocks, became the best known member of a family which also claimed earlier descent from a governor of Dyserth Castle in the reign of Henry II. Madocks was elected as Member of Parliament for Boston in Lincolnshire. He was a man of great vision and enterprise and created the 'ideal' community of Tremadog, which, of course, derives its name from him. But he was also the driving spirit behind the cob between Porthmadog and Penrhyndeudraeth, which was considered to be one of the wonders of the early nineteenth century. It contributed greatly to the transportation of slate later in the century. For a time Madocks had the enthusiastic support of the poet Shelley in the venture, but sudden, mysterious, circumstances made it necessary for the latter to flee Wales.

Another large house in the area has interesting associations. Thomas Wynn, who lived at Penllwyn was one of the auditors of the revenue of Charles I, and his memory is perpetuated on a tablet in the church.

During the early years of this century, the most common cause of death in Wales was tuberculosis. But due to the crusading spirit of a Member of Parliament, David Davies – later Lord Davies of Llandinam – it was resolved to set up the King Edward VII Memorial Association. This was an effort to raise money which could be set aside for medical research and facilities, which would contribute to the fight against this disease. The initial subscription amounted to £200,000, and it therefore became possible to open a hospital specialising in the treatment of TB in North Wales. It was decided that Llangwyfan would be an ideal location, and the hospital opened its doors in 1920, with 226 beds. The opening was to be remembered by many years afterwards, the ceremony being performed by George V accompanied by Queen Mary. They travelled by royal train to Denbigh and by motor vehicle for the remainder of the journey. A civic dignitary welcomed the royal couple at Denbigh station, and the King responded with a pre-written response.

'In reply to your loyal address, we are very glad to visit your beautiful town crowned by its ancient castle so renowned in history, and standing in one of the fairest valleys in the kingdom, and to see around us the thriving and successful agriculture for which the Vale of Clwyd is famous.'

When they arrived at Llangwyfan they officially opened one of the largest hospitals of its kind in Britain.

By the late nineteen forties and early fifties advances were at last being made in the fight against this fatal chest condition, and there was a drop in the number of patients being admitted. Eventually Llangwyfan began to offer treatment to those with other medical conditions of varying kinds. It closed in 1982. Later the site was transformed into a residential community for the mentally handicapped.

Llangwyfan today enjoys a peaceful way of life, but it has no shops or a post office. These provisions are available at Llandyrnog village, which is situated a mere mile away.

Llangynhafal

This small rural community is situated on the B5429, which runs between Denbigh and Rhuthun via Llandyrnog. The widely scattered parish is, even today, a fairly remote one.

The name of the village is derived from a seventh century missionary saint, with the formidable name St Elgud ap Cadfarch ap Caradog Freichfras. The location of the church, which is still frequented by a loyal local congregation, was probably chosen because it was on a well used route which travellers would take in order to cross the Clwydian hills into Flintshire.

Visitors will notice that the roof of the church is of an unusual design, with alternating hammer beams and arch braces. There was once stained glass here, but it was destroyed in the seventeenth century by Cromwell's men who regarded colourful, decorative, church features as being at variance to the Christian faith. This is a perverse attitude which is incomprehensible to us today.

The lectern is designed to represent a pelican, a bird which has great significance in religious terms. It was believed to feed its young on the blood from its breast, and this is interpreted as symbolic of Christ's sacrifice for mankind on the cross.

In our own increasingly secular age it is often forgotten just how intense religious meetings in the past could be. It is reported that at Llangynhafal, when the words 'beat down Satan' were uttered by the congregation, they would give hearty assent with a violent stamping of feet.

Services were initially accompanied by music provided by instrumentalists rather than an organ, and these included a bass, a viol, a clarinet and a mandolin.

The first known Rector was Thomas Plumer, who was appointed in approximately 1390.

A much later Rector was David Lloyd, who was Warden of Rhuthun in the seventeenth century. He became Dean of St Asaph, and wrote his own, very frank, epitaph:

'This is the Epitaph
of the Dean of St Asaph,
Who by keeping table
Better than he was able
Ran much into debt
Which is not paid yet.'

Plas Draw, once the home of Colonel Charles Bromhead

The Pelican in Llangynhafal Church

There is a holy well situated within fairly close proximity to the church, and this is reputed to contain specific healing powers for warts. The wart would be touched with a pin, a prayer would be uttered, and then the pin would be dropped into the well.

Our knowledge of the social history of the parish is derived largely from the contents of a large church chest, which you can still see today. These include churchwardens' accounts and vestry minutes.

In the eighteenth and nineteenth centuries the parish was self-governing and a number of locally elected officers drew up legislation, some of it quite harsh.

A constable was appointed and his duties included the whipping of idle beggars. He had charge of the village stocks, and was also granted the power to remove paupers who failed to qualify for parish relief.

Churchwardens were unpopular figures because they had the responsibility for raising rates, but refusal to accept this office could result in prosecution.

There are some notable large houses in the area. Plas Draw is Georgian and was frequently lived in by tenants. Colonel Charles Bromhead lived here at the beginning of this century. He had been an officer in the South Wales Borderers. It was the Colonel's brother, Gonville Bromhead, a frequent visitor to the Vale of Clwyd, who was awarded the Victoria Cross for his heroism in the Battle of Rourke's Drift, when his men were heavily outnumbered by Zulu tribesmen. This episode was brilliantly portrayed in the 1964 feature film *Zulu*, in which Bromhead was played by Michael Caine.

Plas Dolben is an eighteenth century mansion and its name derives from Robert Dolben, who came to live in the Vale when he was granted Segrwyd, near Denbigh, by Henry VII as a reward for services rendered.

Plas-yn-Rhos is one of the oldest houses in the parish, and a barn bears the date 1612. It was the home of William Wynne, who was appointed High Sheriff of Denbighshire in 1738, the only parishioner to occupy this office until 1981, when Lady Marigold Graham became the first woman High Sheriff of the county.

Plas-yn-Llan is an attractive sixteenth century half-timbered house, next to the church. At the end of the eighteenth century it was owned by Edward Jones, who was a lawyer who practised in Denbigh. He had six sons and daughters, one of these being Robert Jones. While at university Robert became a close friend of one of the greatest English poets, William Wordsworth. Wordsworth is known to have stayed at Plas-yn-Llan on two occasions, and he was evidently impressed by the splendour of Wales. With Jones, he walked to various parts of North Wales. In a letter he writes of 'the sea sunsets which give such splendour to the Vale of Clwyd'.

Evidence of the high regard in which Wordsworth held Jones is contained in these simple lines of verse:

'This picture from nature may seem to depart
Yet the man would at once run away with your heart,
And I for five centuries right gladly would be
Such an odd, such a kind, happy fellow as he.'

*View of local pottery at Llanrhaeadr
from the lychgate of St Dyfnog's Church*

Llanrhaeadr

In a book on parish churches, Sir John Betjeman asks:

'Is there anything in a church worth cycling twelve miles against the wind to see? In the case of Llanrhaeadr there is, and it is a window, the Jesse Window.'

The east window of St Dyfnog's Church is indeed a beautiful example of stained glass. The subject depicted is the Root of Jesse and the ancestors who descended from his lineage. It is not by any means the only Jesse window in Britain, but there can be little doubt that it is one of the very finest. During the English Civil War in the seventeenth century, the window was removed and hidden in a large wooden chest in a hole which had been dug in a nearby wood. Cromwell would have disapproved of the bright colours of stained glass, and would inevitably have ordered its destruction.

During the second world war it was boarded up and sand-bagged against the possibility of bomb blast. In the nineteen eighties a major restoration scheme was carried out at the church, and this involved the window being removed yet again. It was finally replaced during Easter 1989, and the villagers who had been behind this enterprising project were forced to raise a substantial sum to pay for the work which was carried out.

There has been a place of worship at Llanrhaeadr since the sixth century, when St Dyfnog lived. This means that a continuous tradition of Christian worship can be traced back for no less than 1,400 years. There can be little doubt that Dyfnog's choice of this location was determined by the presence of a well, close to the point where the present church now stands. The water was believed to have healing properties.

The oldest part of the present church is the thirteenth century tower. Double aisles, which are a distinctive feature of Vale of Clwyd churches, are to be found. At one time it seems that the roof was thatched and the walls whitewashed. A vivid reminder of the past may be observed as you enter the church, for there are grooves in the stones near the archway which could be the result of locals sharpening their arrows during archery practice.

In the churchyard are some interesting graves. Edward Wynne is buried here, the fourth son of Edward Wynne and the grandson of Maurice Wynne, who was one of the four husbands of Catrin o Ferain. He was in the service of Charles I during the Civil War, and was Captain of Foot in the garrison of Denbigh. He was wounded in a skirmish with

Parliamentary troops who were attacking Denbigh in 1645, and the injuries were so severe that he only lived for a further three days. As his father's house was within the parish of Llanrhaeadr, it was felt that he should be buried in the churchyard there. But the village was beyond the boundary of the King's army and so an agreement was arrived at between the two sides, which resulted in a temporary truce to enable Wynne's funeral to proceed in a dignified way. His remains were escorted by a party of his own regiment to a point on the Rhuthun Road. From this point, Cromwell's men took charge of the body and the cortège wound its way respectfully to the churchyard. Even in the heat of battle, such civilised arrangements are sometimes possible.

In the grounds of St Dyfnog's, you will also find a monument to Anne Parry, who was a devout and God fearing woman who lived at Prion. She opened her house for Methodist services and also started a local Sunday school. Her life was cut short when she was forty-three, and nine years after her death her son also died. Interment was to be within the same grave as his mother, and when the grave was opened up once more, Anne Parry's body was perfectly preserved and without any sign of decay. Even the flowers which had been placed beside her on the day of her funeral were still fresh and fragrant.

Within the church is the splendid white marble monument which was erected to perpetuate the memory of Maurice Jones of Llanrhaeadr Hall, who died in 1702 when he was only thirty. The memorial is a fine example of the decorative ornamental art of his period, and Jones is represented in repose wearing an elaborate wig and handsome clothing. He is attended by two cherubs angels who are both weeping. Jones' widow, who was one of the well known Bagot family, commissioned this striking feature of the church and it was she who endowed the nearby alms houses. Each resident received a weekly allowance, together with a supply of coal and clothing. They are still occupied.

By the end of the eighteenth century Llanrhaeadr Hall, a modest house by the standards of that period, was owned by Richard Parry, who had grandiose plans for its enlargement. These never came to fruition, however, although a new wing was added.

Over the centuries, the well has been mentioned in the writings of visitors. A writer in the eighteenth century, for example, writes that:

' . . . the famous well of St Dyfnog is much resorted to and on that account provided with all the conveniences of rooms, etc., built around it.'

You may still visit the well by following a well defined footpath through woodland close to the church.

Opposite the church is the King's Head, which dates back to the sixteenth century. The atmosphere within is redolent of days gone by and, like the Llindir at Henllan, it is reputed to be haunted by a female ghost. She is thought to have met a tragic death when a stage coach in which she was a passenger met with a violent accident close to the village, in the late eighteenth century. Certain visitors to the King's Head claim to have caught a glimpse of her over the years.

This is not the only unusual feature, for in the bar is a darkly polished carved panel depicting a witch and a warlock. In a dim light the facial expressions of these two characters are said to change.

Since 1970 this part of the village has been by-passed, which means that, in general character, it is now a little more like the Llanrhaeadr of earlier times. The other half of the village is a more recent development and here you will find the community shop and post office, a restaurant and the premises of a motor coach company. There has been a considerable amount of residential development during the last thirty years or so and the instrumental force behind this has been builder Emrys Jones. He designed housing which took account of the rural environment, and believes that other villages should, in future, be more aware of this aspect when homes are erected.

The statue at Llansannan
commemorating some local worthies.

64

Llansannan (Conwy)

Llansannan is situated on the A544 between Bylchau and Llanfair Talhaearn in the Aled Valley, in the region known as Hiraethog.

The church was built on its present site in the thirteenth century, and was largely rebuilt in 1778 and restored a century later. There was once a gallery for a mixed choir. As was the case with most other Welsh churches in earlier times, there would be no evening services held because of the lack of facilities for lighting the church adequately. But the lack of electricity had no effect on chapel services, and their doors were thrown open during mornings and evenings. They would put lumps of clay at the ends of the seats and place candles in these.

There are some interesting anecdotes relating to the chapel culture of the village during the heyday of Nonconformity, a time when new places of worship were opening at a rapid rate.

For example, one of the members at a particular chapel was Joseph Davies, a farmer and cattle dealer. He took some of his stock to Shrewsbury where he hoped to sell them, and while there received news that his wife was very ill. In an anxious state he set off as far as Cerrigydrudion on horseback, but was fearful of venturing any further in the darkness of night in case he met with an accident. He resumed his journey early the following morning, and when he eventually arrived home discovered that his wife was making a recovery. Some members of his chapel took an absurdly dim view of anyone who, for whatever reason, went out on the highways on the Sabbath day, which was when Davies had made much of his journey. They considered that every Christian had a duty to attend chapel, and spend the rest of the day meditating on the Bible at home. They took the extreme measure of expelling him, and as a result Davies, together with a few other members of the chapel who took his side, rallied together and built another Congregational chapel in the village.

In 1848 there was a potato famine, and at a prayer meeting held in Capel Rhiw an old man was on his knees praying intently. In the middle of his exalted thanksgiving he suddenly remembered the scourge of the potatoes, at which he exclaimed angrily: 'Bother it! You've spoilt the bloody potatoes!' He then resumed his normal tone of prayer, while his fellow worshippers viewed him with alarm.

The historian W. Bezant Lowe, to whom we are indebted for our knowledge of the history of the village, thought that the oldest approach via Henllan may indicate the approximate direction of a Roman road between Denbigh and Caernarfon. The Chester to Holyhead mail route passed a little to the north of Llansannan in the eighteenth century. From 1789 this was no longer used, as an alternative road nearer the coast carried passenger vehicles.

A monument in the village perpetuates the memory of some of the great literary figures who had their origins here. One name which is inscribed on this memorial is that of William Salesbury (1520-1584). This remarkable man was educated at Oxford and went on to become one of the leading Renaissance scholars of his day. He saw the need for a Welsh Bible and was instrumental in making this available, although not in a complete form. His work was revised and completed by William Morgan, and between them they made an outstanding contribution to the survival of written Welsh.

Tudur Aled (1465-1525) took his name from the nearby river and was a very highly skilled poet, one of his better known poems being one dedicated to St Winefred. He played an important part in the first Eisteddfod at Caerwys.

Moving forward to the nineteenth century we have William Rees (1802-1883), who used the pseudonym 'Gwilym Hiraethog'. He was a noted writer and also edited a newspaper. He was a chaired bard and wrote a celebrated poem on the Battle of Waterloo. For many years he was the minister of Capel Lôn Swan in Denbigh, and his preaching was characterised by a very zealous manner of delivery. Two American universities conferred degrees on him. He spent his final years in Liverpool, where he died.

One of his less exalted contemporaries was the village bookseller John Davies. He travelled around the villages of the Hiraethog area hawking his books. This was at a time when many country people were only semi-literate due to their lack of early education, while the ones who could read could ill afford the price of books. Bookselling was not Davies' only claim to fame, for he kept a diary in which he recorded his impressions of village life.

The mansion of Dyffryn Aled, which was totally destroyed by fire many years ago, was the home of the Wynne family. One of the family was Diana Wynne, who was born in 1748, and married twice. Her second husband was Philip Yorke of Erddig.

During the first world war Dyffryn Aled was converted into a prisoner-of-war camp for German naval officers. It was from here that a daring escape was attempted, and three prisoners were involved. They were convinced that if a submarine could be sent to the North Wales coast, they would be able to escape and rendezvous with it. As it happened a fellow prisoner was being sent back to Germany through the exchange of prisoners scheme, and through him they conveyed a message to the naval authorities of their home country. Somehow or other instructions were eventually received and on a specified evening they made good their escape, dressed in civilian clothing. They arrived at Llandudno the following morning, and went into hiding on the Great Orme for the rest of the day. They remained there until evening but emerged under cover of darkness and began making their way in the direction of the beach. As arranged they got their flashlamps out and proceeded to signal out to sea. However, there was no response at all. Desperate by this time they ventured into Llandudno, and were soon apprehended by the police and taken into custody. Afterwards it emerged that the submarine had been close at hand the whole time, but had been hidden from view by a rocky headland. If their plan had been successful they would have been the only German war prisoners to have escaped from Britain by submarine during the 1914-18 war.

Nantglyn's unusual feature; a pulpit set within a yew tree.

Nantglyn

Nantglyn lies some four and a half miles from Denbigh, fairly close to the Hiraethog moors. It is thought that it may have been on a route taken by medieval pilgrims on their journeys to Bardsey Island. For the farmers, the availability of suitable upland grazing land within close proximity of the Nantglyn area proved very practical, and in the eighteenth century two fairs were held there every year.

Little seems to be known about the origins of the community. Being situated in a sheltered spot, with good water and land, it may well have been a settlement from early times. Tradition has it that Nantglyn had a resident saint, St Mordeym, in the sixth century. Although it is known that the priest at Nantglyn in 1284 was Dafydd ap Llywarch, nothing is known about the church at that time. The present church dates from the late eighteenth century, but underwent additions and alterations during the Victorian period. One unusual feature at St James' is a massive yew tree which has an open air pulpit built into it, consisting of lime and stone. As far as I know, no other North Wales church has a similar feature. In the eighteenth century John Wesley is thought to have preached an open air sermon here to a large crowd.

Nantglyn has had its fair share of talented men, and these have all enriched the cultural life of Wales.

David Samwell, who was the son of a vicar of the parish, was a considerable scholar, and he pursued a medical career. He is best remembered today as the surgeon who sailed with Captain Cook on his final ill-fated journey to the South Seas. He witnessed, and later wrote about, the murder of Cook by hostile natives in Hawaii.

Thomas Edwards, more popularly known as Twm o'r Nant, was a colourful character and the author of dramatic interludes. George Borrow, the author of *Wild Wales*, thought very highly of him and writes about him at length in the book, describing him as 'The Welsh Shakespeare'. He is buried at Whitchurch in Denbigh.

William Owen Pugh, a Meirionnydd man, lived there during the later part of his life. He produced an awful English-Welsh Dictionary, the result of painstaking effort and patience. His son Aneurin was a fine scholar.

In his *Book of North Wales*, published in 1903, Sabine Baring-Gould claims that the famous eighteenth century actress Mrs Jordan was born in Nantglyn, but in her biography Claire Tomalin has completely disproved this. One of the graves to be found in the churchyard at Nantglyn is that of a man named Foulke Owen. The manner of his death is extraordinary, and has as its setting the high moorland region of Hiraethog within a few miles of the village.

Foulke Owen was engaged to a girl named Janet, but jilted her in order to marry a girl from a wealthier family. He and his wife went to live at Tyn-y-Gors, to the south of Hafod Elwy. One winter night, when the snow lay thick on the ground, Foulke walked to Denbigh on business. His route took him along what was once a medieval road, crossing Pont y Brenig. When he failed to return home it was decided that a search should be organised. This resulted in the discovery of a few of his personal possessions along the way. It therefore seemed likely that Foulke had perished and was lying somewhere under the snow, but no trace of his body could be discovered. Further searches failed to throw any light on his disappearance in the following weeks. In the meantime Janet, who was employed as a maid at a farm in the area, dreamt on two consecutive nights that she was working with Foulke in the hay harvest in a field near Cerrig Caws, a distinctive hill to the west of the Brenig Reservoir, which is reputed to have been the site of a medieval market. The weather was extremely hot, and Foulke, growing weary, decided to have a rest.

'I'm going to lie down on that bank over there,' he said to Janet. 'When I'm asleep I want you to cover my face with my jacket to keep the sun out of my eyes.'

Janet found this dream disturbing, and her mistress insisted that she should visit the Owen family in order to relate it to them. With the Owen family she eventually went to Cerrig Caws, and Janet pointed to the field bank where, in the dream, Foulke had fallen asleep. With their hands they dug beneath the snow and soon found his body, with the jacket over his face.

His burial is recorded in the Nantglyn church registers and his son, who was born only a few weeks after his death, is also buried there. Foulke's widow went on to marry a man named Davies. When the late Bill Wynne-Woodhouse was the Chief Ranger at the Brenig Reservoir in the nineteen seventies, he was visited by people from Canada who are direct descendants of this second marriage. Through family conversations they had learned of Foulke Owen and the sad circumstances of his death.

Nowadays the undulating road from Denbigh bears only local traffic and the lifestyle of the village is unhurried and relaxed.

It no longer has a shop, although the post office has been retained. You will look in vain for a pub here. In the nineteenth century there were three but the last one closed in 1928.

The agricultural and flower show always attracts visitors from a wide area, and in the past Nantglyn has been awarded the Best Kept Village Award in the former county of Clwyd.

Like other North Wales villages, it was self-sufficient in the eighteenth and nineteenth centuries, and something of that independence lives on today.

Pentrefoelas (Conwy)

Pentrefoelas is situated on the A5 between Cerrigydrudion and Betws-y-coed. The surrounding area once incorporated land that was granted by Llywelyn Fawr to the Abbey of Aberconwy in 1195.

Before the monasteries were dissolved in 1541 a chapelry was located in the village, and this was administered by the incumbent of Ysbyty Ifan, which came within the overall rule of Aberconwy Abbey, Maenan. Services were subsequently taken by lay readers, and the resident priest from Ysbyty Ifan administered the sacrament twice a year. An increase in the population meant that a new church had to be built in 1766, and much of the financial support for the new building came from the Wynne family of Voelas Hall. A vicar was finally appointed when the village gained parish status in 1810. There was no burial ground attached to the church, therefore the dead were buried at Ysbyty Ifan or at Llannefydd, the parish of which once included Pentrefoelas.

In the mid-nineteenth century the church underwent major structural changes, and the building that we see now is, to a great extent, the result of the design of the famous clerical architect Gilbert Scott. The cost was again borne by the Wynne family. An east window perpetuates the memory of one of the family, who was killed in the Crimean War in 1854.

Records of nineteenth century life, and death, survive. Between 1842 and 1852, for example, there were one hundred and three burials, and of these twenty were children under the age of three. The crime rate was low, and between 1850 and 1857 only two parishioners were gaoled for theft. Inbreeding was largely the result of a lack of geographical mobility. The people were insulated within their community, and this was further intensified during the winter months when heavy snow often enveloped the Hiraethog area.

The non-conformist movement grew in this part of Wales in the early nineteenth century. Azariah Shadrach was one man who worked

71

A general view of Pentrefoelas

fervently to ensure that the church did not impose a monopoly of religious worship. He began by preaching on the bridge in the village. It is also reported that he indulged in face-to-face preaching on the doorsteps of dwellings around the village, and it was even claimed that he made payments to some people in order to induce them to listen to what he had to say. Although he was the object of much hostility, he built up a considerable following, and as a result the Independents established a Sunday School. The Calvinistic Methodist Chapel followed in 1815, and was regarded with hostility by the established Church.

In 1857 there were some forty different trades and occupations being carried out in the village, and a poem of that period mentions all of these. They include the publican, shopkeeper, draper, saddler, blacksmith, carpenter, bookbinder, tanner, priest and doctor.

The village was a gathering place for cattle. Here the beasts would be herded together by drovers before proceeding to the shoeing centre at Cerrigydrudion.

The Foelas Hotel was originally a farm. It was granted a coaching licence in 1839, and both the Royal Mail and Stage Coach service would stop there on the London to Holyhead run.

The area has a rich cultural history, and in 1849 a village Literary Society was established. When you consider the extreme limitations of the elementary education which its members had received, it is remarkable that so many should have become so very talented in both the composition of poetry and prose.

In 1919 the first village Eisteddfod was held, and proved extremely popular. It took place on nine subsequent years, and in 1922 no less than 9,000 attended, to hear Madam Leila Megane singing at an evening concert. The Eisteddfod was forced to discontinue because of lack of funding.

In 1931 the present school opened, combining primary and secondary education. It was the first school of its kind to open in North Wales.

Up to about fifty years ago Pentrefoelas was a thriving community, but villagers have since been forced to move to other areas in search of employment. During the nineteen eighties a serious attempt was made to halt the decline, and due to the sponsorship of various organisations, the abandoned greystone buildings, formerly the workplaces of tradesmen, were restored. They were then opened again by craftspeople, and a heritage trail was routed to enable visitors to get the most out of a visit here.

Llannerch Hall, Trefnant

*Unlike so many of the North Wales churches
the one at Trefnant is fairly recent in origin.*

74

Trefnant

Situated on the A525 between Denbigh and St Asaph, Trefnant is a Victorian village that began to evolve in the eighteen-fifties. The church was built at the time when the Vale of Clwyd railway was under construction, and was designed in the Gothic style which was fashionable then. It was originally conceived to perpetuate the memory of Colonel and Mrs Salusbury, members of a local landed gentry family. There was no previous church in the immediate locality.

Many of the farms that flourished in the area some sixty years ago have now disappeared. At that time the railway facilitated the transportation of animals and produce. An elderly man recalled the small village station as a scene of bustling activity, where cattle, sheep and timber would be loaded on to freight trains three times a week. The cattle usually went to Chester market.

In 1908 Mary Heaton, who lived in Trefnant, decided that it would be a good idea to revive 'the old jointed toys as a means of giving employment and interest to the working men of Trefnant in the winter'. She was the daughter of the Rev. H.E. Heaton of Plas Heaton, Henllan. Between 1910 and 1912 a total of seventy men took advantage of the opportunity to learn the skills of toy making. Although the first toys were not very sophisticated, a selection was sold at a Welsh industries exhibition in London. The venture was made possible through the financial assistance provided by Denbighshire County Council. When they withdrew support Miss Heaton was forced to look elsewhere, and she found an ally in the Duchess of Dundonald. A model of the Gorsedd for the National Eisteddfod was produced in 1914, and by that time the toys from this little Welsh village were sold in various parts of the world. Miss Heaton's enterprise was rewarded, and she was directly responsible for the toy industry being sanctioned as the first Rural Industry Training Centre in the country. Soldiers who had been wounded in action were billeted at her home, Bryn Hyfryd. These servicemen welcomed the opportunity to learn new skills, despite their sometimes severe physical disabilities. Lloyd George visited the factory in 1918 and is said to have been impressed. Sadly, in 1920 the factory was forced to close due to the cheap toys that were arriving in this country from abroad. Mary Heaton was awarded the O.B.E. in recognition of her efforts.

Within fairly close proximity is the former Llannerch Estate, where deer once grazed the extensive acres of lush fields. In the Tudor period, Peter Mutton lived here who's father, William, was a burgess of Rhuddlan. The mansion remained in the possession of landowning families in the eighteenth and nineteenth centuries. One landowner felt that a railway station should be constructed at Llannerch to serve the estate, which was a good example of the self importance of gentry families in the nineteenth century. The railway company refused to comply.

Ffynnon Beuno Cave, Tremeirchion

Tremeirchion

Tremeirchion is situated to the south east of St Asaph and the name of the village derives from the personal name, Meirchion, the original dwelling being his homestead.

The church has a unique claim to fame in that it is a medieval parish church still dedicated to Corpus Christi. The original structure is thought to have been thirteenth century, although it seems likely that there would have been a wattled hut, or a cell, on the site as long ago as the sixth century.

In the fifteenth century additions and renovations were carried out, and a north transept was added in the nineteenth century. The parish has had some notable vicars. The Rev. John Roberts, who was born at Llannefydd, was the vicar at Tremeirchion from 1804 until 1840 and in 1815 he introduced the very first harvest festival in Britain. The Rev. Hicks Owen was another nineteenth century rector and was married to Harriet, sister of the famous poet Felicia Hemans, who lived at St Asaph.

Unfortunately the church lost two items of immense historical interest. One was a Celtic Cross, which was reputed to have miraculous powers and was known about throughout Wales in the sixteenth century. It seems that it fell into neglect and was eventually sold by the church authorities for £5. Another misfortune befell the old parish hearse when, in 1950, it was burned by people who had no conception of its historical value.

The church has a gallery where, in times gone by, musicians would have sat to accompany the hymns during services. In the churchyard are some ancient yews, some well over 800 years old.

Ffynnon Beuno is a greatly renovated house with an important history and there are three different facets which make it so interesting. One is the well, which is close to the house. It is some four feet deep and the water runs constantly, bubbling up from the ground. It had the reputation for the cure of eye troubles in mediaeval times.

A further focus of interest are the two caves, which can be found in a field beyond the house and the well, Ogof Ffynnon Beuno and Ogof Cae Gwyn. Both have yielded evidence of prehistorical life and these take the form of animal bones, including the hyena, the mammoth and the lion. In the nineteenth century the caves were a great local tourist attraction. In the *Denbighshire Free Press* in June 1886 we read:

'The caves will prove a great attraction during the present season. Members of the Chester Geological Society say that they are more interesting than even the famous Cefn Caves.'

Ffynnon Beuno was a tavern in the nineteenth century. When Denbigh-born John Rowlands, later to become H.M. Stanley, absconded from the parish workhouse at St Asaph, he stayed here for a time with an aunt. In his autobiography he describes this period of his life in detail and recalls some of the work which he, very willingly, carried out for his keep.

'I trimmed hedges, attended the sheep, fed the stock, swept the yard, drove Dobbin to Rhyl station for coal or to Denbigh for beer.'

Within close proximity to Ffynnon Beuno is Brynbella, a large mansion, which became the home of Hesta Lynch Piozzi, a significant eighteenth century figure. Her maiden name was Salisbury and she was one of the Bachygraig branch of the famous Llewenni Salisburys. Her first husband was Henry Thrale, a London brewer, but after his death, and much to the disgust of Dr Johnson, she married Gabriel Piozzi, an Italian dancing master. Brynbella was built for them and the name combines both the Welsh and the Italian. She loved the house and wrote of:

' . . . my beautiful new residence built for me in my own lovely country.'

Before she died in 1821, Hesta Lynch Piozzi expressed a wish to be buried at Tremeirchion, and a fine tablet within the church perpetuates her memory.

Her ancestral home was Bachygraig, situated a mile or so from the village on the Denbigh road. This was used by Edward, the Black Prince as a hunting lodge in the fourteenth century. The farm house which we see today was once part of a considerably larger building and is steeped in history and myth. It is reputed to be the first brick built house in Wales since Roman times, the bricklayers having been brought from Holland by Sir Richard Clough, whose home it became. It was, by the standards of its period, spectacular in design and no fashionable tour of northern Wales by the cream of English society was complete without a visit. Some of the locals, however, considered it to be the work of the Devil! Clough had a keen interest in astronomy and would spend hours on end during the night on the very top floor with his telescope projecting through the roof towards the galaxy.

Also close to the village, in the direction of the A55, is St Beuno's College, which was erected in 1848 as an institution for the training of Jesuit theological students. It was probably sited here because of its comparative closeness to the shrine of St Winifrede at Holywell. Nowadays St Beuno's is a spiritual retreat centre, but in the days when the training of prospective priests took place here the way of life was rigid and self-disciplined.

In 1874 Gerard Manley Hopkins, who was destined to become one of the finest English poets commenced his three year training period here. Some of his best remembered poems were written during this time and he has also left us impressions of some of the places in the area in his unique letters and journals. The supreme beauty of this part of the Vale of Clwyd is wonderfully encapsulated when he writes of:

'... the woods, waters, meadows, combes, vales,
All the air things wear that build this world of Wales.'

Slate headstones at St Mary's Church, Bagillt

Flintshire

Bagillt

Bagillt overlooks the Dee estuary and is located off the A548 between Mostyn and Flint.

When industrial development was changing both the physical landscape of the area and the lives of the people in the eighteenth and nineteenth centuries, Bagillt was a focal point of activity in terms of north-eastern Wales as a whole. It was located on a productive coal seam, had two large lead smelting works, and a rope making factory. A quarter of the lead produced in Britain was transported to Flintshire to be smelted in the village. But in the eighteen forties an unlikely form of employment came to the area with the establishment of a company that made straw hats.

It is not surprising that the population of Bagillt grew quickly, when one takes into account the amount of commerce and industry which was becoming an integral part of life in that corner of Wales. English industrialists found it a sensible location for their enterprises, with its very close proximity to the Dee and the comparative nearness of Liverpool. Small fishing boats had been using Bagillt for centuries, but the industrial revolution ensured that the village developed into a port with a number of quays.

A pier was constructed in the late eighteenth century in order to transport coal from the Coleshill Colliery Company's works. This was superseded when the main docks close to the station were built. Before long Dee Bank Quay was also built to serve the Dee Bank works at Bettisfield Colliery.

The earliest references to Bagillt's importance as an industrial port are contained in the papers of the Gadlys Lead Company in the seventeen thirties. The doos, which included lead and calamine, were transported to larger sailing vessels. Ancillary activity were attracted, including a foundry, a brewery, and an engineering works. Houses were, of course, needed to accommodate employees, and the second half of the nineteenth century led to the opening of shops, public houses, and other commercial premises, while there was work as milliners, tanners, blacksmiths, and a large number of other trades and occupations. A local industrialist was noted for his benevolence to his workers and this contributed to a feeling of mutual cordiality.

The brewery referred to was owned by William Pierce and was

opened in 1825, but went out of business seventy-five years later. Pierce lived in some style in a house called 'Oaklands'.

The workers from the various factories and other businesses would enjoy their hard-earned leisure hours drinking at local taverns. But in 1879 the Bagillt Cocoa House and Workingman's Institute opened as part of a nation-wide movement to reduce the problems brought about by alcohol.

Bagillt declined in importance when, in the twentieth century, there was an economic depression. Deeside, generally, lost its place as a region of importance as far as maritime trade was concerned.

But Bagillt was not only a busy commercial centre in the nineteenth century, but was also on a tourist route. We find Worral's Directory of 1874 describing the community as 'a large thriving village'. This was the age of the pleasure-steamer, and passengers were conveyed by coach from Liverpool to Hoylake or Parkgate, and then over the estuary to the Flintshire shore. Regular sailings took place, thus providing pleasant day trips for visitors. One vessel 'The Duke of Lancaster' was met at Bagillt by horsedrawn vehicles. These took passengers on to Holywell, St Asaph and Denbigh. The Ship Inn served as a booking office. Other steam-packets which did the run over the years were 'The Ancient Britain' and 'The Cambria'. In 1895 this service came to an end, and a much quicker journey was available by rail with the opening of the line between Wrexham and Secombe.

At one stage of his life Thomas Pennant owned Bagillt Hall, but demolished it because of:

' . . . the thick smoke of a great smelting mill for lead and of a great calcining-house for calamine just beneath which must ever deter my descendants from making it their residence.'

Paul Panton was born at Bagillt in 1727. He was a close friend of Thomas Pennant and, like him, travelled widely in Britain in search of antiquities. When he moved to Ynys Môn he took a leading part in the cultural life of the region. In 1749 he became a barrister. Another Bagillt men who became a barrister was Enoch Salusbury, who was called to the bar in 1852. Later he became a Member of Parliament for Chester.

It is not as a legal man or a politician that he is primarily known today, however, but rather as a collector of books. He had a very large library of titles relating to Wales, and in 1880 published a work called *Border County Worthies*.

Edward and Joseph Williams also hailed from Bagillt. They were brothers who became well known in Wales in the early part of the nineteenth century as singers and harpists.

George Tattum lived in the village and produced verses which, although lacking in any real literary merit, were enjoyed by an unsophisticated readership. In them he refers to the social changes which were taking place during his lifetime.

The Buckley Silver Jubilee clock situated on the former town hall.

Buckley

Buckley is located on high ground above the Alun Valley, three miles east of Mold.

Although it has been administered by a town council since 1974, its evolution was that of an industrial village. In the Postal Directory of Flintshire and Denbighshire (1886) it is described as a 'large and prosperous village', while in Sutton's Directory of North Wales (1889-90) it is summed up as 'a large and extensive village'.

Although coal was extracted here, it is chiefly for its pottery that Buckley is known. Pots have been produced here for the last six hundred years, and from the medieval period until the nineteen forties there was a continuous tradition of pottery in the village. Today all that remains to reveal the working places of the potters are overgrown claypits, cinder piles and workers cottages.

Pottery has served both a functional and decorative purpose. We don't really know when clay was first used to make pottery but it certainly seems likely to have been utilised for this purpose before the birth of Christ.

It is not possible to ascertain when pottery was first made in Buckley, either, but John le Potter and Philip le Potter were each named in subsidy rolls dating to 1292. They could well have been among Buckley's first potters.

Buckley Mountain potters produced goods for a fairly select market and worked in small family groups for three centuries.

By the seventeenth century the potter had become an important figure in the local community, and there was a never ending supply of local clay for his requirements. Improvements to navigation on the Dee estuary, around 1737, meant that new marketing possibilities could be explored. This resulted in wares which were less expensively priced, and a new lease of life for exports. Thomas Pennant, writing in the seventeen eighties, wrote of:

. . . very considerable potteries, which make annually between three and four hundred pounds worth of pot.'

Fourteen potteries supplied goods to London, Ireland and the Welsh ports. During this period there was a growing demand for bricks, and potters began to manufacture these. By the seventeen nineties, six works were entirely given over to the production of bricks. In 1822 four large companies made over seven million bricks. By 1835 brick-yard and pottery employees worked a twelve hour shift each day, six days a week.

Some companies, such as Powell's, introduced partial mechanisation, colour glazing techniques and other innovations. Most were family businesses where one family would own and work a pottery for generations; the Catheralls and the Hancocks for example. At one point, in 1818, no less than three hundred workers were employed by the Catheralls.

But the nineteenth century saw the beginning of the end of pottery at Buckley due to competition from cheap Staffordshire china, a decrease in trade to Ireland, and the consequent closure of many factories.

But in its day the village was something of a cultural melting pot as men from Lancashire, Staffordshire and other regions arrived to take up work. This stimulated the development of ideas, and the mixture of immigrant accents resulted in the unusual and distinctive English dialect spoken by Buckleyites, as they have become known.

When the Commission of Enquiry into the State of Education in Wales took place in 1847 the authors had this to say of Buckley:

'All the children of Buckley speak English, but with a strong provincial accent which would be as difficult to correct as it would be to teach English to Welsh children.'

In his novel *Rhys Lewis*, Daniel Owen makes one of his characters ask:

'Do you at Bala talk like they do at Buckley tell me?
Little bit of Welsh and little bit of English mixed.'

J. E. Messham, a local historian of renown, writes:

'I suppose there has been a Buckley dialect for at least six hundred years . . . Out of many diverse parts an isolated community fashioned over generations a dialect which was unique in its blend of words and pronunciations.'

Buckley's annual Jubilee began in 1859. Children from different Sunday schools would march through the village singing hymns and accompanied by a brass band. Clergymen addressed the crowds, and after a lavish tea the children played games. Traditionally this was held during the second Tuesday of July, and shops and factories would close for the celebration. Old Bulkeyites from all over Britain still return to be present at this event. A Jubilee clock is situated at the old public library building.

Interest in Buckley ceramics has undergone something of a revival in recent years, and James Bentley has been a key figure in giving the potteries a high profile. In addition to being the greatest living authority on the Buckley dialect, he has also built up a substantial collection of both artefacts and documents relating to community history. He has also painted scenes of Buckley life in days gone by and written his personal reminiscences.

Sir Ben Bowen Thomas, who hailed from the Rhondda region, felt that Buckley had a strong affinity as an industrial community with industrial communities in his home area:

'Buckley and Rhondda may have lacked neon lighting but they glowed from within. They were both spontaneous and exciting communities. Experience was vivid. Events were on the march.'

The tower of the church of St Mary the Virgin, Cilcain

Cilcain

Cilcain is located four miles west of Mold, and is seven hundred feet above sea level and within close proximity to the Alun Valley.

It is thought that St Eurgain, the daughter of Maelgwn Gwynedd, retreated to this area when she was in danger of being persecuted because of her Christian convictions in the sixth century. She had a hermitage here which later became the site of a church. In the Norman period the church was rebuilt, and the building which we see today, St Mary's, is the focal point of interest among the buildings in the village. It has a double nave and during the eighteenth and nineteenth centuries was substantially altered, as indeed were so many churches in Wales and England. The tower dates from the sixteenth century. It is surrounded by a circular wall, and from the grounds fine views may be obtained of the Clwydian Hills. It seems likely that the carved hammer beams came from Basingwerk Abbey in Greenfield following the dissolution of the monasteries.

A traditional Christmas morning Plygain service was once a tradition here. The service would begin in the early hours of Christmas day and usually included appropriate portions of prayer, with or without an address, and unaccompanied carol singing by either parties of men, often local farmers, or individuals. Everyone who attended brought with them their own candle with which to lighten the darkness of the church. In 1532 a candle was the cause of a fire which burnt down the north aisle after a service.

The vestry books contain a number of interesting items. There were, for instance, frequent purchases of the rushes with which the church floor would be covered, as well as heavy expenditure on the extermination of polecats and foxes. The skilled services of a mole-catcher were also much in demand.

In 1762 the first Methodist meeting was held on a nearby hillside. As far as we can gather, prior to this, groups of worshippers would walk along the local lanes on Sunday evenings singing hymns.

Red Lion Yard, as it was then, was also a meeting point for Methodists. On one occasion an itinerant preacher was delivering a sermon there when another man, who was an enemy of Methodism, climbed on to the roof of a nearby building with the intention of dropping a stone on the preacher's head. But a man who had come along to listen to the sermon is reported to have spotted the miscreant and to have bawled a threat at him, to the effect that he would kill him if he dropped the stone. This had the desired affect.

When John Speed the cartographer visited the village in 1610 he wrote of the well, Ffynnon Leinw, which he claimed ebbed and flowed in a tidal fashion.

There was once a smithy here, built in 1572, with an external staircase.

Opposite the church stood the old school house and, as was so often the case, the money to cover its running costs and maintenance would be the result of the good will of subscribers.

The one remaining inn is the 'White Horse', which opened in the sixteenth century. Much of its custom at that time came from horse-drawn coach travellers. In the nineteenth century there were no less than seven inns in the Cilcain area.

Edward Jones (1761-1836), the hymn-writer, who was a native of the Denbigh area, lived at Cilcain in the latter part of his life, and died here.

An ancient trackway will take the walker over the Clwydian hills to Llangynhafal, a distance of some three miles. It is an exhilarating walk on a fine day.

Basingwerk Abbey, Greenfield

Greenfield

Greenfield is situated on the A548 coastal road between Rhyl and Merseyside. As you drive through today you will see an unremarkable community, which does not even have the virtue of having a particularly rural character. But historically Greenfield and its environs have considerable importance in the history of Flintshire.

Basingwerk Abbey, which can be found very easily, and is now administered by CADW, is thought to have been founded by Ranulf, who was an earl of Chester in 1131. It was modelled in its design on Savigny Abbey in Normandy. Over a century later it became allied with the abbey at Buildwas in Shropshire.

In 1188 Gerald of Wales spent a night at Basingwerk with Archbishop Baldwin when they were travelling through Wales obtaining recruits for the Crusades. He described:

' . . . a district where there is a rich vein of silver and successful mining works, and where, by delving deep, they penetrate the very bowels of the earth.'

This is yet a further indication of the importance of the area in terms of its mineral deposits.

While the Welsh wars of the thirteenth century were taking place Basingwerk favoured the English cause.

Later in its history it was visited by itinerant Welsh bards. The abbey offered patronage to Gutun Owain. He was a very notable poet of his period and became a popular figure at the abbey. He actually wrote about the life of Basingwerk in some of his poems, and the impression he creates is of an affluent institution where the Abbot gave twice the measure of wine to his guests, which even a king would not have done. Other evidence also adds to a general impression of luxurious living. It seems that the principles of celibacy and self-denial were being flouted.

Following the Dissolution of the Monasteries in 1536 Basingwerk became the property of the Mostyn family, but by that time it was estimated that its value amounted to a mere £158.

In the late fourteenth century the industrial activity of the area declined, but in the seventeenth century it again assumed an importance in the local economy. By the early years of the eighteenth century factories had been built in the Greenfield valley. One of these was described by the literary tourist the Reverend Richard Warner:

' . . . The mill till within recent years employed one thousand people, but the same paralysing effects of war have been produced here as in other manufactories throughout the kingdom, by the reduction of their numbers to five hundred women and children.'

Thomas Pennant described conditions at another mill in glowing terms, and here is his description of the living accommodation of the children apprentices:

'The cotton twist company have between three and four hundred apprentices, which they feed and clothe themselves in commodious houses built for that purpose. All the windows of the sleeping rooms are open at the tops, by which a thorough draft of air is admitted during the time the children are at work. To these and other precautions the good state of health of so many children may be justly attributed. Their food for dinner is beef, or pork, and potatoes . . . as much as they please to eat. A surgeon is appointed to superintend their health.'

This account would seem to be deceptive, and it seems almost certain that Pennant was relying not on his own personal observations but on a description conveyed to him by the factory owner concerned. But the poet John Jones (1788-1858) provides us with the harsh voice of experience. He was a child labourer in one of the mills, and his writing gives the lie to Pennant's comments.

Well I remember, how in early years,
I toil'd therein, with unavailing tears . . .
No bondage state – no inquisition cell,
Nor scenes yet dearer to the Prince of Hell,
Could greater acts of cruelty display
Than yon tall factories on a former day;
E'en neighbouring forests frowned with angry nods,
To see, Oppression! thy demand for rods!
Rods doom'd to bruise in barbarb'rous dens of noise
The tender forms of orphan girls and boys!
Whose cries – which mercy in no instance foun'd,
Were in the din of whirling engines drown'd.
But all is past, and may Treffynnon see
No more of fell Prestonian tyranny.

The reference in the final line is to John Smalley, the factory owner, who was a native of Preston. Jones succeeds in making us vividly aware of the sheer human suffering which resulted from the exploitation by employers of a poor, half starved workforce.

Although the Factory Act of 1833 restricted the employment of children, the mill owners at Greenfield flagrantly ignored this for the simple reason that it was less expensive than paying for adult labour. Today the Greenfield Valley Heritage Park occupies the ground where foul fumes were once belched forth from dark mills and factories. This enterprise was realised in 1971, when it was felt that the wilderness of tangled undergrowth which had spread over the area should be cleared for a constructive purpose. In this process, on more than one occasion, the skulls of children were discovered within the ruins of former workplaces.

Today the site is attractive and pleasant, giving the public an understanding of the industrial and agricultural history of Flintshire, in a woodland setting. A complete farmhouse has been lovingly re-erected, stone by stone, from its original location on the lower slopes of Moel Fama, and a barn has also been moved to the site. It dates from the last century. The Spring Garden School, a Victorian building from Holywell, has also been painstakingly restored. The very rigid educational routine which children would have experienced is recreated by today's youngsters for the benefit of visitors.

In the late nineteenth century, the construction of a railway line between Greenfield and Holywell facilitated the transportation of locally produced goods. The ascent was quite daunting. 'The gradient was one in twenty,' a local man explained to me, 'which meant that if you were in the town cinema, the vibrations caused by the train going by would make the screen go one way, while the picture went another.'

The most important employer in Greenfield in the twentieth century has been Courtaulds. They opened their factory here in 1916, and produced a fibre from cellulose, or wood pulp. This was used either by itself, or blended with other fibres. They also produced sulphuric acid, which was used in the manufacture of rayon.

'It was a vast factory,' an ex-employee told me. 'It was the largest rayon factory in the world, and employed 1200 men during the war. It was producing items for the war effort, such as parachutes. It was a community within a community really, and the companionship and friendship was great. When I first started there it was really hard work, but automation came eventually, which made it easier. We thought automation was a great thing at first, but it wasn't in the end, of course, because men began losing their jobs because machinery could do it more economically'.

I also talked with an ex-railwayman in Holywell, and wondered whether he had any particular memories of Courtaulds.

'Well, of course the full employment is missed,' he responded, 'but what we don't miss here in Holywell is the stench that used to come from the place. The fumes were vile, and as a railwayman I recall the brass buttons of my uniform turning black if the wind was in a particular direction.'

Courtaulds also had factories at Flint, the Castle Works and the Deeside Mill.

A stop at Greenfield to visit both Basingwerk Abbey and the Greenfield Valley Heritage Park will give the visitor an insight into the fascinating, if sometimes disturbing, past of this apparently nondescript village.

The Eagle and Child outside the seventeenth century inn
of that name in Gwaenysgor

Gwaenysgor

Gwaenysgor is situated above, and inland from, Prestatyn.

Of all the village churches in Flintshire, St Mary Magdalene has probably changed least. It was last rebuilt following the war between Prince Llywelyn and Edward I and its appearance is not unlike the way it was then. The combination of ancient grey stone, some very old tombstones, and a conservation scheme to allow the flora and fauna to flourish here, make the church well worth a visit. As you walk around you really feel as though you are taking a step back in time. A feature of the building, which is very characteristic of the medieval period, is the large south porch with a stone seat running around the walls. It could have been a meeting place for the settling of disputes, petty trials and other village matters.

The parish records seem to be the only completely unbroken records of a Welsh parish, and they date from 1538. In the churchyard is a sundial which is dated 1663.

Situated in many churches were doors known as 'Drws y Cythraul' *(The Devil's Door)*. It is possible to detect where this was located at Gwaenysgor. This door was specifically for the benefit of people who had not been baptised or had been excommunicated. Babies were also admitted through the door when christenings took place, but immediately after any of these had crossed the threshold into the church, the door was slammed shut to keep the Devil out! When an excommunicated member of the congregation had repented of his misdemeanours and shown remorse, he could be re-admitted to the church through this door. The Norman font has a bowl rim on which are deep grooves, where daggers and swords could have been sharpened on the stone. The warriors believed that by using the font for this purpose they were endowing themselves with strength and virtue.

There is a lepers' window dating from the fourteenth century, which would allow those unfortunate enough to be afflicted with this terrible disease to listen to the service from outside the church, and to receive the sacrament.

A corpse bell, used three hundred years ago, stands on the window of the south sanctuary. It was the custom for it to be rung by a man who preceded funeral processions as they were on their way to the church.

The old well in Well Lane supplied water for the village up to the period of the First World War, when standpipes were installed. Water was not made available to every household until after the Second World War.

The first school was established in a building now known as Craig yr Ysgol. Later, a church school was established. The children of non-conformist families were educated in the vestry of Rehoboth Chapel. In 1908 a new school was built, but this closed in 1967 and is now the village hall.

The area is one to which archaeologists have gravitated over the years and Gop Hill is fairly close to the village. There is information about this site in the chapter dealing with Trelawnyd. Offa's Dyke also runs close by.

An Elizabethan mansion called Golden Grove was the family home of the Morgan's. During the Civil War in the seventeenth century they were staunch Royalists. Captain Morgan and his men engaged a large party of Parliamentarians in a skirmish, and the Captain lost his life. It seems that he was buried on the north side of Llyn Helig. According to the antiquary William Davis writing in the nineteenth century:

'The grave was opened some time ago by a person wholly unauthorised by the family; the armour had partially decayed, but a silk skull cap was found in a state of great preservation.'

The name Golden Grove derives from the fact that a line of fine trees stand in that area.

A view of Halkyn

96

Halkyn

Halkyn is situated off the A55 between Holywell and Hawarden, and the known history of the area dates back to Roman times. They were quick to realise the potential of natural mineral resources, and mined for lead.

By the time the Romans left Britain mining activity was minimal, and it was not until the arrival of the Normans that the mines became fully active again. In the thirteenth century the miners were granted certain rights and became 'free miners'. They drew up a charter, one object being to deter trespass and theft at the mines, and there were very harsh penalties for those who transgressed. Some offenders were pinned to a post, with a dagger through their hands to suffer a slow and excruciating death.

Timber was necessary for smelting purposes and other needs, and this resulted in the abundant woodland which covered Halkyn Mountain being dramatically reduced. In order to maintain a basic subsistence miners were also forced to keep a few cows, sheep or pigs.

In the fourteenth century the Black Death swept through the area and resulted in the death of countless families. Others fled in an attempt to escape the ravages of the terrible disease. After this there was a decline of mining activity until the first half of the seventeenth century. In this period Sir Richard Grosvenor was granted the rights of mining in Halkyn by Charles II. There were soon five mines operating and apart from lead, limestone was also extracted. Thomas Pennant observed:

> We have had at different periods mines productive of vast wealth in several parts of this tract. The richest vein was discovered about fifty years ago at Pant y Pwll Dŵr on Halkyn Mountain which, in less than three years, yielded to different proprietors, adventures and smelters about a million in money.'

But there was much poverty among the common people and the unhealthy working conditions lowered the resistance to disease and illness. Pennant describes 'a cruel kind of quinsy' which gripped the people of Halkyn, especially young children. In what may have been a potent form of lead poisoning, the afflicted would push out their tongues 'like an overheated dog'. Charities for miners who were injured or fell sick were established but were administered in very questionable ways, and substantial sums of money were unaccounted for.

During the Napoleonic wars there was something of a decline in lead mining and it was not until peace was regained that it began to resume its former importance.

The Grosvenors built Halkyn Castle between 1824 and 1827, replacing an older building. They stayed there on many occasions up to 1913, when it ceased to be used. It was an important part of their Flintshire estate.

The population of the area fluctuated according to the success of the mines, but in 1858 the village was flourishing; seven taverns, two cobblers, two blacksmiths, three general provision shops, a tailor and a number of other businesses fulfilled local needs.

The church of St Mary was rebuilt in 1877-8 by the Duke of Westminster and has been described by a leading architectural historian as 'one of the best Victorian churches in Clwyd'.

A church was established at Halkyn prior to the Domesday Book in 1086, and it seems likely that it would have occupied ground close to the site of the present church.

Some of the clerics who have been associated with the history of the church were colourful characters. A rector of the fifteenth century supported the rebels of Owain Glyndŵr. In the mid-seventeenth century Rhys ap John was dismissed from his rectorship for selling pardons and relics. A vicar of Llanasa in the fifteenth century attempted to bribe the Bishop of St Asaph for the more lucrative parish of Halkyn. The Bishop, it seems, was not beyond temptation.

Dr Rowland Williams was born at Halkyn in 1817 and became a distinguished academic. He was educated at Eton and Cambridge, developing a passion for the study of linguistics. This led to him being appointed Professor of Classics at Cambridge, a post in which he remained until he secured the professorship in Hebrew at St David's College, Lampeter.

He was one of several contributors to a publication called *Essays and Reviews*, published in 1860. The established church violently opposed many of the views expressed by Williams and he was the subject of condemnation. His case was dragged from one ecclesiastical court to another until, eventually, he was found guilty. But he appealed and this resulted in a ruling in his favour. He spent his final years living near Salisbury and continued to write prolifically. His poems included one called *Prince Madog*, which is based on the traditional belief that Madog ab Owain Gwynedd discovered America in 1170.

Hawarden (Penarlâg)

Hawarden is situated on the A556 six miles west of Chester. Following the construction of Offa's Dyke in the seventh century, Hawarden became a part of the Kingdom of Mercia. A century earlier than that, Conan was an influential leader in North Wales, and during his lifetime a Christian place of worship is thought to have been established here. The focal feature was a rood-loft surmounted by an image of the Virgin Mary. A tale, which may well be apocryphal, relates how during a summer of exceptionally severe drought the desperate villagers went to the church in order to pray for rain. Among them was Seisyllt, the wife of a local worthy. As she prayed the image of the Virgin Mary fell on her; and she was killed. It was therefore decided that the image should be removed and placed on the sands beside the Dee. The tide took it out and it was eventually discovered at Chester.

The remains of the motte and bailey castle have become known as 'the old castle', as they stand within the grounds of the impressive and more recent Hawarden Castle. This was the home of the great Victorian statesman William Ewart Gladstone, who is strongly associated with Hawarden.

In the Domesday Book the old castle is referred to as the chief manor and capital of Alticross. This encompassed an area which extended from the Dee to the Vale of Clwyd. The castle belonged to the English crown in 1205, but was attacked by Dafydd ap Gruffudd, brother of Llywelyn, in 1282. The castle was recaptured, and following this conflict it was rebuilt of stone.

During the English Civil War it held out for the Royalists, but was finally captured by Cromwell, who ordered that the castle should be destroyed.

The surrounding parkland was bought by John Glynne, who became a Lord Chief Justice. It was a descendant of his, Catherine Glynne, who married Gladstone in the parish church. They made their home at the 'new' Hawarden Castle, upon which work had begun in 1752. Many years later Sir Stephen Glynne commissioned Nash, who also designed Buckingham Palace, to work on the architectural designs which were to transform it into the building we see today.

It was in the nineteenth century that the old castle became incorporated into the parkland which also includes the 'new' castle.

Gladstone took a great sense of pride in the land surrounding his fine home. He was a muscular man, and tree felling became his favourite form of relaxation from the cares of office. It was during the felling of a

St Deiniol's Library, Hawarden

*William Ewart Gladstone. Detail from the memorial
to the family at Hawarden.*

tree that the summons came from Queen Victoria asking him to form his first government in 1868. An eye-witness described the scene in these words:

'Mr Gladstone in his shirt sleeves was wielding an axe to cut down a tree. Up came a telegraph messenger. He took the telegram, opened it and read it, then handed it to me, speaking only two words, 'Very significant', and at once resumed his work.'

He was extremely popular with the villagers, and one old woman reverently kept a fragment of wood that had flown off a tree which he had felled. She kept it in a glass case in her parlour and would proudly point it out to all who visited her. Towards the end of Gladstone's life, Hawarden became a place of pilgrimage for his many admirers from far and wide. When the gates of the park were opened in 1874, people gravitated to this corner of Wales in their hundreds, and the opportunist staff in the estate office sold Gladstone wood chips for charity. Special trains ran to Hawarden, and on one of these seven hundred members of the Ladies' Shamrock League of Liverpool descended on the parkland. People lined the roads when the grand old man went to church, and an image of his head began to appear on plates and mugs.

In 1889 Gladstone purchased three acres of land, and on this he built what was to be a temporary library. He arranged for 27,000 books to be transferred from his own collection. Within a few years students were staying at a nearby house while they undertook their studies at the library.

Following Gladstone's death it was felt fitting that a new memorial library should be erected, and this resulted in the building of the St Deiniol's Residential Library, a unique institution to which both students and scholars come from all over the world each year in order to research their chosen subjects.

Next door to the library is what was the rectory, a fine Georgian building which now houses the archives department for the whole of Flintshire, a further centre for research.

The church has undergone considerable restoration and you will find a window perpetuating the memory of Gladstone, which was commissioned from Burne-Jones. There are also effigies of the great Prime Minister and his wife.

Another well known person with associations with the village is Lady Emma Hamilton. Her maiden name was Hart, and during her childhood years she lived at Hawarden for a time with her grandmother.

Today Hawarden is a neat village of red sandstone houses, a broad main street, and its general appearance is suggestive of an English rather than a typically Welsh village.

Part of the east window at Llanasa Church

Llanasa

This peaceful village, situated off the A548 between Prestatyn and Mostyn, lies in a rural setting. It has a village pond, a feature not all that common in Wales.

It seems that the community had its origins in the sixth century, when the second bishop of Llanelwy built an early place of worship here. The present church dates from the early sixteenth century and is double naved. Anyone visiting the church will be struck by the magnificence of the stained glass in the large east windows. It was brought from Basingwerk at the time of the Dissolution of the Monasteries, during the reign of Henry VIII.

There is a sepulchral slab set in the floor on which is inscribed the name of Gruffudd Fychan who was the father of Owain Glyndŵr. He is thought to be buried in the church. A commemorative memorial plaque was erected to the memory of the Gronant lifeboat crew who perished while bravely attempting to save the lives of others, drowned in 1857.

In the eighteen seventies there were a number of trades in the village; a general grocer, a boot maker, a draper, a blacksmith, a baker and a book seller among them. A woman named Ann Cartright was evidently an extremely industrious woman; she farmed sixty acres, ran the 'Red Lion' and delivered the mail. In the second half of the nineteenth century, the lead mines and the limestone quarries provided employment for many local men.

The village had some interesting nineteenth century customs. Elias Owen tells us that Easter was a season which was joyfully celebrated, and there was a custom of 'heaving' during this celebratory period. On the Easter Monday young men, accompanied by a fiddler, went from house to house, the object being to 'heave' the young women. Any girl who did not receive a visit took this as a snub. On the Tuesday the girls went out in force to return the compliment. Owen does not tell us what 'heaving' actually consisted of, but it was some kind of courting ritual. He also records a custom in the village of distributing seed cakes on All Saints' Day, to the poor, who would then pray to God to bless the next crop of wheat.

No account of Llanasa would be complete without a few words about John Jones, who was referred to in the chapter on Greenfield. He was one of the very few Welsh-born poets writing in English in Wales in the nineteenth century. Born in 1788 he came from a very poor family, and was put to work in a cotton factory in the Greenfield Valley at the age of eight. In his poems he wrote graphically of the terrible working conditions which children were forced to endure. In 1804 he joined the navy for nine years and served on warships in the West Indies, Spain, Finland and France. He returned to a life of working drudgery in Holywell, but some years later moved to Stalybridge in Cheshire where he lived for the rest of his life. He was known to his English neighbours as 'Poet Jones' and sold his poems on the streets. When he died a very large number of mourners attended his funeral service.

Elis Gruffydd was a minor country gentleman who was born in Llanasa in 1490. He lived at a time when the Tudor dynasty was on the throne, a good period for enterprising and well-to-do Welshmen. He is known to have entered into the service of the Wingfield family in London. In this capacity he travelled to Calais for a while. For four years he was the Steward of Sir Robert Wingfield's mansion in London. In this capacity he did a great deal of scholarly work, including the transcription of ancient Welsh literary texts. In 1529 he returned to Calais as a soldier and spent the remainder of his life there. (He is still remembered as 'the Soldier of Calais').

He wrote a book in which he chronicled the history of the world up to the time when he was writing. In it he writes:

'This I caused to write down that the matter be not forgotten in Llanasa.'

There is a further literary link with the area, for close to Llanasa is the hamlet of Glan-yr-Afon. For a time this was the boyhood home of Emlyn Williams, the actor and dramatist. His parents moved to Glan-yr-Afon when he was an infant of three months old.

As you approach Llanasa from the direction of Gwespyr you will find yourself close to the 'Old Hall' (*Henblas* in Welsh). Work on this mansion began in 1645 and as with many large old rural houses, there is some folklore relating to it. Every so often, a team of horses could be seen driving through the gates, and for anyone who happened to witness this sight it was predicted that bad luck would follow. On one occasion a man is said to have visited the village to stay with friends. As he was walking along the road towards the Red Lion one day he caught a glimpse of the coach and horses going up the drive to the 'Old Hall'. When he got to the pub, what he had witnessed was very much on his mind, and it occurred to him that possibly a film company were making a costume drama in the area. When he returned home the man died suddenly. Of course there may well not have been any connection at all between what he claims he saw and his sudden death, but – as in all stories of this kind – one is left wondering. During the Second World War the 'Old Hall' became an internment centre for German prisoners of war.

There is a plaque in the church which reads:

'To the honour and glory of God and in memory of Frank Nicholson, organist and choirmaster of this church who died on October 28th 1928.'

Nicholson had been employed as a carpenter at Talacre Hall, and he possessed a fine baritone voice. He competed at Eisteddfods with great success, and regularly broadcast on BBC radio in the twenties. The people of the village were proud of his achievements and Lord and Lady Mostyn were among his keenest admirers. On his way to work one day, singing a song which he wished to memorise, he took a short-cut over the fields. While doing so he was attacked by a stallion and killed. It struck him to the ground and stamped on him. This tragedy shocked and saddened villagers and a postcard was produced showing Nicholson's coffin being conveyed into Llanasa church.

No account of the village would be complete without a note on Gyrn Castle. It had been owned by Roger Mostyn in the early eighteenth century, but passed to the Rev. Samuel Edwards on his marriage to Charlotte Mostyn. In 1853 it became the property of Edward Bates, who became Member of Parliament for Plymouth. He was a shipping merchant, and became a baron in 1880.

'The Honest Man' sign outside the Lletty Hotel, Mostyn

Mostyn Docks

Mostyn

Mostyn is situated on the A548 between Rhyl and Connah's Quay. The commerce of this Deeside community has traditionally been associated with the transport of goods by sea, and it has therefore assumed a significant role in the maritime history of north-east Wales. But if we go a good deal further back in time, we discover that a manor house stood on the site of what is now Mostyn Hall during the time of the Welsh chieftains. The Mostyn family claim their descent from these leaders, and affiliated themselves closely to the House of Tudor.

When Henry VII was making preparations for the overthrow of the House of York he moved around Wales in order to summon support for his cause. Many of the Welsh were pleased to offer their services to him, as Henry's grandfather Owain Tudur of Penmynydd, Ynys Môn was a man whom they greatly respected. (No less than 1,600 Flintshire miners marched to Bosworth with him.) Henry visited Mostyn. A lavish meal was prepared in the main hall but just as the guests were about to sit down, news arrived that a party of Yorkists were on their way to capture Henry. He made good his escape by jumping through a window and escaping through an underground tunnel.

The lord of the manor at that time was Richard ap Hywel, and he threw himself into the battle at Bosworth with great bravery for which he was awarded by Henry with the belt and sword which he himself had worn on the field of battle.

During the seventeenth century Sir Richard Mostyn defended Flint Castle for the Royalists. A contemporary wrote describing him as ' . . . a gentleman of good parts and metal . . . in twelve hours he raised fifteen hundred men for the king'. He was victorious in the taking of Hawarden Castle, but was later taken prisoner at Chester.

Thomas Pennant tells us that when Rowland Lee was the president of the Marches in the reign of Henry VIII, he wearied of the number of Welshmen with whom he had dealings whose names included ap, or son of; as with Thomas ap Richard ap Hywel ap Ieuan Fychan. This name he, in the words of a contemporary document, ' . . . reduced to the poor dissyllable Mostyn, no doubt to the great mortification of an ancient line'.

By the early sixteenth century the area was becoming industrialised, and two London entrepreneurs wished to establish a lead-smelting mill. Although they were granted official permission to do so by the Privy Council, Piers Mostyn opposed them vehemently. He had no wish to tolerate what he felt would be an evil-smelling mill so close to his fine home. William Mostyn, his son and a Justice of the Peace, began to think of ways in which the mill might be destroyed as it was being built. Mostyn gathered around him some eighty men and they quickly set about demolishing what had been built, with a good deal of violence. Much acrimony ensured and Mostyn had to appear before a high court in London.

In the fifteenth century coal mining was growing in importance as a source of heating for large houses and castles. Pack horses would carry coal down to the Dee, and from Mostyn it would be transported by marine vessels; some to Rhuddlan, Conwy and Beaumaris. Later it was sent to Dublin for the more affluent citizens of that city.

Coal has always had an important role in the economic history of the area, but mining was an immensely hard way of life. Inevitably accidents sometimes occurred, and there were a number of lucky escapes. In his fascinating book *A Second Walk Through Wales* published in 1798, the Reverend Richard Warner writes:

'Not more than two or three years ago, the roof of a mine in Mostyn park so suddenly gave way that a poor workman, not having time to escape, was instantly overwhelmed with the foundering earth. Standing fortunately at this time under a mass of rock he escaped being immediately crushed to death; but as there were a thousand tons of earth above him, the melancholy prospect of certain destruction by means of the most lingering and terrible death still presented itself to him. When the accident happened, he had half a pound of candles in his hand, and upon this, and the trickling water that distilled through the cracks of the rock, he subsisted nine days, until his faithful companions at length reached and liberated him from the horrible prison in which he was immured.'

We also have evidence of a boy of ten who, while out at play, fell down a mine shaft three hundred feet deep, and survived with very few injuries.

In the seventeen forties malnourishment and starvation became rife in Flintshire, the cause being a particularly bad series of harvests. This led to mob rule and rioting and many men from Mostyn were involved. With men from other areas of the county they marched to Denbighshire, and by the time they arrived at Rhuddlan their ranks had been swelled by some 1,300 people. They ran amok and seized wheat wherever they could find it. Troops were brought in, in an attempt to quell an explosive state of affairs but, none the less, a good deal of fighting continued and a number of people were injured.

The parish is not an ancient one, for it only came into being in 1844. Prior to this it had been a part of the neighbouring parish of Whitford.

Christ Church was completed in 1844 at a cost of over four thousand pounds. It was erected to meet the spiritual needs of people who were moving into the community in order to find work, for it was an area which was burgeoning because of its location at a key point on the Dee estuary. A variety of goods were exported including coal and bricks, the latter having been manufactured in Buckley. But the Dee could be extremely treacherous as Charles Kingsley's poem *The Sands of Dee* makes clear. In his book *Shrouded Quays* Aled Eames relates the sad fate of Captain Bennett, master of the 'Taliesin'.

'One stormy night, with the tide ebbing, the 'Taliesin' was anchored close to the shore and the captain had gone ashore to get his orders. He started walking along the sand, but in the wind and rain the crew lost sight of him after seeing him opening an umbrella to shelter a little from the weather. The captain disappeared for ever, but the crew discovered his open umbrella on the sand the following morning.'

In 1904 Mostyn had a population of no less than 1,642, and men were arriving here to find work in the coal industry. It was once claimed, with how much truth it is difficult to know, that at one time there were as many coal shafts in the village as there are days of the year. Local mining records go back to the sixteenth century, and if you add to mining the other industries situated in or near Mostyn, it quickly emerges as a very significant area in Flintshire. The Mostyn Coal and Iron Company was established in the nineteenth century. In the early part of the century there was a considerable demand for pig iron to supply the foundries of the munition factories during the Napoleonic war period. A copper works, slag recovery, ship building yard and brick works all flourished within close proximity to each other.

In July 1884 the Mostyn Colliery was forced to close due to the fact that the waters of the Dee had broken through into the workings. Initially coal was transported to Mostyn from the pit at nearby Point of Ayr, three miles away, but later it was being obtained from wider afield. The opening of the Chester to Holyhead Railway in 1848 meant that the transport of goods from Mostyn was made much more smoothly, and it was not long before sidings were built connecting the main line to the docks.

The coming of the railway saw the demise of the passenger-carrying paddle-steamers. You will have already have read a little about these in the earlier chapter on Bagillt.

Over the years the Mostyn Company owned no less than fifteen sea-going vessels, and it was a busy port. The docks still has a reputation for its transport facilities, and nowadays the quays are well equipped with electronic cranes.

Not very far from Mostyn is Lletty Hotel, which was once a pub called 'The Honest Man'. According to various accounts the 'honest man' was called Smith and he lived in the seventeenth century. One night while staying in Chester he dreamed of building an idyllic tavern in the country. The dream must have made a great impression on him for the following day he determined to act upon his nocturnal flight of fancy and set out on foot for the Mostyn area. Here he quickly discovered a suitable spot for an inn, and when the building work was complete he set about furnishing it. But, very mysteriously, he then disappeared and no one ever saw him again. It seems that any owner of an inn who left it free of debt was in those days regarded as a truly honest man, and a stone was inscribed to commemorate his memory and placed above the door. It is dated 1699.

Fairly close to Mostyn today you will see, as you drive along the A548, a pleasure cruiser known as the 'Fun Ship'. It was towed to its present berth in the nineteen seventies, and was concreted down in order to make it secure from the estuary tides. It is a tourist attraction and situated close to the site of a regular Sunday market.

Robert Davies was a generous local benefactor. He came from a long line of Mostyn seafarers and acquired his wealth from his maritime activities. In 1925, at considerable personal cost, he built a fine hall for the use of local people and this became known as the Robert Davies Memorial Hall. A notable feature is the external clock. The building remains in use as a venue for various events.

Northop (Llaneurgain)

Situated on the busy A55 between Holywell and Hawarden, Llaneurgain derives its name from a female saint from the sixth century, Eurgain, who is thought to have been a niece of Elwy (St Asaph). The Saxon invasion which took place in about the year AD 828 resulted in this region of Wales being defeated by King Egbert. This resulted in many of the Welsh place-names being replaced by Saxon ones.

This has been a site of Christian worship here since the time of Eurgain but it was not until approximately 1200 that a stone church was erected. It was extended two hundred years later in order to incorporate additional features, including a vestry.

In the sixteenth century the central arcade was added. Work also took place on the fine tower, which is ninety eight feet high. Margaret Beaufort, the mother of Henry VII was a benefactor, and without her it probably would not have been built. Following her death in 1509 there was a shortage of finance which could be spent on the church.

The nineteenth century was a flourishing period in church restoration, as other references in this book make clear, and the work carried out has enhanced the appearance of the church which we see today. Three recumbent effigies can be seen within, two of knights in full armour from the late fourteenth century. One we can identify as Ithel ap Bleddyn, the husband of a lady represented in the third of the effigies.

Part of an ancient window is set in the wall of the churchyard, and this was the east window of the original church. It was removed during the restoration.

Within the churchyard you can see the still sound structure of the old Grammar School, which dates from the sixteenth century. In its time, it was considered one of the most important schools of its kind in Wales.

In the age of the stagecoach, Northop became the first stopping point for coaches commencing their journey from Chester to Holyhead. Villagers would frequently be disturbed at three o'clock in the morning by the sound of the post-horn and horses.

Doctor John Wynne was buried at Northop in 1743. He was born at Afonwen and became Bishop of St Asaph, the first time that a Welshman had been appointed to that position for one hundred and fifty years. He later became Bishop of Bath and Wells. You will also find the resting place of Owen Jones here. He was another generous benefactor of the church and in the seventeenth century gave one hundred and five acres of both land and property in the village, for the benefit of the poorer people. As a child he was left by uncaring parents within the tower of the

The old grammar school, Northop

The church at Northop

church, where he was discovered by the verger attached to the bell-rope. The parish took him into its care, and he eventually prospered and became a butcher in Chester.

Northop was the birthplace of William Parry, a Member of Parliament during the Elizabethan period. He was a zealous Catholic during a period when religious allegiance was a highly emotive issue, and was involved in a plot to assassinate the queen. When this came to light, Parry was executed. He claimed that he was a member of the Conwy family of Bodryddan, and that his father had died at the age of one hundred and four years after fathering no less than thirty children by two wives.

The village has some importance in the history of Wesleyanism in Flintshire largely due to the activities of Richard Harrison, who devoted his efforts to the teaching of Wesley's doctrines in Welsh. Adherents would meet at his home to hold services, a license having been obtained to do so in 1799.

He had a fine singing voice and devoted every waking hour to the propagation of his faith. In 1802 the Welsh Wesleyan Chapel opened in Northop, and in 1804 Welsh Sunday Schools began. More than thirty similar chapels had been built in Flintshire within thirty years of Harrison's death.

As you speed by the present-day Northop, it is difficult to imagine the village in past times, when it was an important market centre. There is some evidence to suggest that the village and its environs were on coal-bearing ground, but as there were no working seams in the immediate area, it escaped industrialisation.

It is thought by some that a Roman road may have run close to the village, and to the west lies a part of Watts Dyke. Next time you are heading along the A55 why not pull off the road to look at the village?

Pantasaph – the arched entrance to Calvary Hill, Pantasaph

Statue of a Fransiscan friar at Pantasaph

Pantasaph

Pantasaph is two miles west of Holywell. Until the nineteenth century it was an obscure, remote community which had been ravaged by quarrying and mining. But in the eighteen forties it was plunged into a fierce theological conflict which ended in litigation.

This was brought about when Rudolph, the eighth Earl of Denbigh, married Louisa, the heiress of David Pennant of Downing Hall, who owned a good deal of Flintshire property, including Pantasaph. The couple were both members of the Established Church. Such was their adherence to their religious ideals that they decided to build a church at Pantasaph, the nearest church being over two miles away at Whitford. They sought the approval of the Bishop of St Asaph and he gave his consent. On a summer's day in 1849 the foundation stone was laid, preceded by a service at Whitford which was attended by a number of church dignitaries. The Archdeacon of Chichester delivered the address.

This was taking place at a time when the religious life of England was being tested to the limit, and when the Established Church was forced to take into account a strong wave of Catholic feeling. The driving force behind this transition was Cardinal Newman. He persuaded many to change ranks from the Established Church to the Catholic faith, and among those who were tempted were Lord and Lady Denbigh. In a sense this was not a very wise decision on their part, especially when they made it known that the church which was in the process of being built at Pantasaph would be a Catholic place of worship. This led to bitter controversy with the Bishop of St Asaph and legal action followed. The Bishop maintained that the church had been given to the Established Church, and could not be alienated. Lord Denbigh became the object of scorn in some of the newspapers of the day, which conducted a vicious campaign against him. At Holywell and Mostyn his effigy was burned in the streets by angry crowds. In our own largely secular society it is difficult to imagine the deep feelings which came to the surface in such matters. Despite everything, Lord Denbigh achieved what he had hoped for, and the well known architect Pugin undertook the design work of the Catholic church at Pantasaph, which opened on October 13th 1852, and was consecrated by Bishop Ignatius Persico.

Lord and Lady Denbigh subsequently spent a good deal of time in Italy, and became attracted to the Fransciscan Friars of the Capuchin Reform. They felt that a similar community should be located at Pantasaph and there happened to be some friars of the order in London at the time. These were poor Irish people who lived in the hope of being able to live together as a community worshipping God. Lord Denbigh offered them Pantasaph and its twenty-four acres of land. They arrived in October 1852 and formed the first community, an important landmark in the Catholic history of North Wales. They toiled hard with pick and shovel to make the bleak, hard ground productive, for they were completely self-sufficient. Initially they were accommodated in the rectory-house. Not long after their arrival Lady Denbigh died in Naples, and her bereft husband clung more strongly than ever to his religious convictions. In 1857 he re-married, and his new wife laid the foundation stone of the monastery.

Lord Denbigh himself lived until 1892 at his family seat in Warwickshire, but he was buried at Pantasaph.

Some years ago the large community building was badly damaged by fire and was not repaired. Close by is a beautifully wooded hill on which a footpath takes the visitor on a gradual ascent to the Stations of the Cross. Countless pilgrims walk up to Calvary at the summit every year.

Between 1892 and 1897 the poet Francis Thompson lived in Pantasaph. He rented a cottage in the village which later became the post office. Being a Roman Catholic he made some friends at the monastery. One of his contemporaries who visited him there was Coventry Patmore, a well established, although nowadays obscure, poet. Following his period at Pantasaph, Thompson lived an existence of poverty and illness in London. He died in 1907 at the age of forty eight.

A little way behind the Convent is St David's well. According to folklore St David, St Asaph and St Cenderin were overtaken by the darkness of night here, and at the time it was a wild and desolate spot. As they were parched with thirst, David prayed; and his prayer was answered. The spring, which is now known as St David's well, bubbled at his feet. Before Pantasaph was provided with piped water, this well was widely used by people in the area. It seems that a local farm always used it during the process of churning butter.

Talacre and Point of Ayr

Talacre is situated off the A548 road two miles from Prestatyn. The village is a recent development, but the square mile of its location is of interest historically. A branch of the Mostyn family have played an important part in the history of this area.

The family rank as the most influential in the history of Flintshire, but the fact that there were two branches is frequently overlooked. Many will know of the Mostyns who gave their name to the village just a few miles away, but fewer are aware of the Talacre Mostyns.

Both families claimed their descent from two brothers, Thomas Mostyn and Piers Mostyn, who both laid claim to an ancient pedigree going back to Tudor Trevor, Earl of Hereford, in the tenth century. The most apparent difference between the two branches lies in their conflicting religious persuasions. The Mostyns of Mostyn abandoned their adherence to the Catholic faith during the Reformation, whereas the Mostyns of Talacre never changed course. There were times when they suffered for their faith, but even then they did not waver. One of the family became the Catholic Bishop of Menevia earlier in this century.

A school was built on the Talacre estate in 1859, for the purpose of educating the children of Catholic families. It was not a popular move as far as many of the local community were concerned, including Welsh-speaking non-conformist.

In his autobiography, Emlyn Williams recalls being a pupil there at a young age. At the start of each day the children would chant:

'Children must never be lazy'
On to work and up si daisy.'

It ceased to be a school before the last war.

The link with the Mostyns came to an end in 1917 when the tenth Baronet died at the age of twenty one. In order to settle the very heavy death duties which resulted, it was decided to put the house and the entire estate up for sale in 1919. This included the land upon which the Point of Ayr colliery stood. Twenty-five Benedictine nuns moved into the Hall in 1920, and its name changed to Talacre Abbey. Some years ago they left Talacre and moved to a smaller establishment in Chester.

Point of Ayr is the area between Talacre and Ffynnongroyw, and the Welsh name is Y Parlwr Du *(Black Parlour)*.

Point of Ayr lighthouse was built in 1777 and was operated by candle light with reflecting mirrors. In the nineteenth century this system was

Point of Ayr Colliery

The view from Talacre looking out towards the lighthouse

replaced by the Dee lightship, which guided countless trade vessels from Liverpool Bay into the Dee Estuary, to the ports at Mostyn, Connah's Quay, Shotton, and Queensferry. By 1988 the lighthouse had been converted into a private residence.

In the eighteen nineties eight horses would launch the Point of Ayr lifeboat and these were loaned by local farmers. There was a tragic event in 1857 when the Irish schooner 'Temperance' was reported to be in severe difficulties off Abergele. The lifeboat set out on a mercy mission in an attempt to save the men on board, but as they got nearer their own vessel capsized. For a time they clung to the side but eventually the sea claimed all thirteen of them. The men whose bodies were recovered were buried at Llanasa, and a plaque within the church commemorates their bravery. In 1923 the life boat service terminated, and in their honourable history they had saved 476 lives.

When the Point of Ayr colliery closed in 1996 it brought to an end the main source of employment in this coastal region of North Wales. There has been mining in this area for centuries, and in the nineteenth century one of the Mostyn family disputed the right of an organisation called The Prestatyn Colliery Company to extract minerals. He laid his own claim to the mining rights, which he argued were on his estate. This led to much acrimony which dragged on for some time, and eventually the Prestatyn company became bankrupt.

The history of the Point of Ayr colliery really began in 1865 when the first boreholes were sunk, but it was not until some years later that good quality coal was produced. It was brought to the surface with the aid of seventy five pit ponies, which spent their working lives underground pulling carts. Many Flintshire men and their families were dependent on the pit for their livelihood and, as one might expect, there was a great feeling of camaraderie among them. This emerges very strongly from the pages of Einion Evans' autobiographical work *Nearly A Miner*, which, despite its modest title, is much concerned with his working life at the pit, and with the close-knit communities from which his workmates came.

In the nineteen eighties, under the Thatcher government, the mining communities came under threat, her policy being to close pits on economic grounds. This resulted in bitter militant action in 1984 when miners came out on strike on a nationwide basis. When they did eventually return to work, they did so with the feeling that they had experienced blatant injustice.

Pit closures continued during the remainder of the decade, but despite talk of the possible closure of Point of Ayr the mine somehow managed to keep going. But in July 1996 came the final announcement of the closure, which took place a month later.

Industrial history is still being made in Point of Ayr, and two months before the closure a major development took place there. It was described by one newspaper as 'one of the very largest industrial projects seen in Wales' and involved the establishment of an oil and gas field in the area. The gas is being piped by PowerGen.

Talacre nowadays offers a complete and utter contrast to every other village represented in this book. It is a highly commercialised Spanish-style holiday centre of rather fragile looking bungalows, caravans, cafes and bars. Beyond it you may walk over the beach in the direction of the lighthouse or, in the opposite direction, towards the now lifeless colliery workings. This area is frequently visited by bird-watchers, as many varieties of sea birds may be observed here.

Gop Hill, Trelawnyd

Trelawnyd (Newmarket)

Trelawnyd is situated on the A5151 between Rhuddlan and Holywell. The dominant topographical and historical feature of the area is Gop Hill, which is within close proximity to the village and consists of a Neolithic cairn and some caves.

The discovery of the importance of the site was made quite by chance by a farmer in the nineteenth century. In the eighteen eighties the Victorian antiquarian Professor Boyd Dawkins sunk a shaft through the centre, and then drove two, thirty foot long, tunnels along the surface of the bedrock. He discovered the bones of various animals which had long ceased to exist in Europe, including the hyena, and also hunting implements and tools. They all indicated that a community had lived and died on the hill in very ancient times. The date of the earliest tool has been estimated at 36,000 BC, a period so chronologically removed from our own that it is difficult to comprehend the huge timescale involved. Another major dig took place in the nineteen thirties, and this added to existing knowledge to some extent.

Gop Hill is a popular site for picnickers nowadays and this is hardly surprising because of its pre-historic interest, but also because of the fine panoramic views which await those who make the ascent.

In the eighteenth century a local landowner, John Wynne, had visions of Trelawnyd becoming a thriving market town. As a result he was instrumental in creating the name Newmarket. He established a weekly market and annual fair, and some trades flourished for a time. These included tanning and hop cultivation. He promoted the non-conformist cause, endowed a charity for apprentices, and proved to be a most enterprising man. Inspired by the Newmarket in England, Wynne also ensured that the village became a horse racing venue. The subdivision of a county or shire, having its own court, was known as a hundred, and such an assembly met in the village, up to the nineteenth century. But Trelawnyd failed to assume the size of a town, despite Wynne's zeal.

The parish church of St Michael stands in a spacious churchyard on the south side of which stands an elegantly sculptured cross, which probably dates from the thirteenth century. It is described by Elias Owen as:

'. . . one of the few nearly perfect churchyard crosses in Wales.'

It is very difficult to put even an approximate date on church crosses. They were the meeting points from which the early missionaries spread the Christian word.

One of the most prominent features in the village, apart from the church, is the memorial hall which was built to commemorate the soldiers of the parish who fell during the 1914-18 war. When news was announced that the war had ended, the school bell is said to have rung until the rope broke. Each year on the anniversary of this occasion, children from the village march to the memorial hall to pay tribute to the bravery of those local heroes. Today the hall is the busy meeting place for the various groups and societies in Trelawnyd.

Trelawnyd has a well known male voice choir and the general area has been drawn on by Emyr Humphreys in his fiction. He was born at nearby Prestatyn and brought up at Trelawnyd. His writing has ranged from novels, short stories and poems, to radio plays. *The Taliesin Tradition*, which can be described as a history of Wales with particular emphasis on its literature, is a magnificent work.

Whitford (Chwitffordd)

Whitford is located two miles from the Dee estuary, between Mostyn and Holywell. It is on the north side of a small valley, so that the road from the south rises steeply at the crossroads in the village.

The church of St Beuno and St Mary may stand on the site of a church built in the seventh century by St Beuno. In the present building the north aisle is sixteenth century. The remainder, including the tower, is from the nineteenth century. The font dates from 1649.

There is a stout parish chest which dates back to pre-Reformation times. One of the two lych gates has an unusual feature in the form of a room over the archway, accessible up an external staircase.

In the south aisle a memorial perpetuates the memory of Thomas Pennant, the antiquarian and scientist, whose name is associated with the area. Moses Griffiths is buried in the churchyard. He is described as an 'ingenious self-taught artist' and accompanied Pennant on his tours of Wales. His illustrations perfectly compliment Pennant's text.

Within the church we are also reminded of 'the faithful servant of Thomas Pennant' Louis Gold 'a Norman by birth'.

Of all the parish histories about Wales, one of the very finest is, without any doubt, Pennant's *History of the Parish of Whitford*. He conveys some memorable insights into the social life of his period. He write of Whitford church:

'I step into the churchyard and sigh over the number of departed. In no distant time, the north side, like those of all other Welsh churches, was, through some superstition, thought to be occupied only by persons executed, or by suicides. It is now nearly as much crowded as the other parts.'

In the nineteenth century a cross was unearthed in the churchyard as a new grave was in the process of being dug. In his informative book *The Old Stone Crosses of the Vale of Clwyd* Elias Owen writes that:

' . . . it was most likely a sepulchral or memorial cross, marking the spot occupied by the dead . . . It is difficult to account for its being buried . . . very little can positively be said of this stone, but the probability is that it belongs to that class of monoliths which are commemorative of the dead.'

Canon Ellis Davies lists no less than twenty sinecure rectors over the centuries. Interestingly they include the names of two individuals who made their mark on the world of English literature. Philip Sydney was

Maes Ychwyfan, the Whitford Cross

appointed in 1564 by Queen Elizabeth when he was only ten, while George Herbert was appointed to this position by Charles I. In principle, the business of appointing sinecure rectors was morally wrong for, as often as not, those chosen did not need to set foot inside the parish and were certainly not expected to do any work.

Maen Achwyfaen is an old stone cross, certainly one of the finest in Wales, and is situated a mile west of the village. It has been there for well over a thousand years and is the tallest wheel cross in the British Isles. The Celtic detail on the inscription, with its fine ornamentation, makes it well worth visiting.

Thomas Pennant lived at Downing Hall and one of his ancestors, another Thomas Pennant, was the last Abbot of Basingwerk Abbey before the Dissolution.

Many think of Pennant only in terms of Wales, and his classic account of his tours around the northern counties in the eighteenth century. But his work was recognised on an European basis, and he contributed a number of papers to the Philosophical Transactions of the Royal Society of Upsala and made his mark, not only in the field of antiquarian studies, but also in the field of zoology. He enjoyed a long and fruitful correspondence with, among others, the Swedish botanist Carl Linnaeus, Gilbert White of Selbourne, as well as such Welsh friends as the Morris brothers of Ynys Môn. He was regarded by many as among the half dozen most significant figures in the intellectual life of the late eighteenth century; Goethe was another. Writing of his *Tours in Wales* one writer commented:

'Pennant made known to the average Englishman a country which had hitherto been as unknown as central Africa.'

Downing Hall fell into ruins many years ago, and hardly a trace of, what must have been, a very fine house now remains.

Whitford differs from many other areas of Flintshire in that no mineral deposits were discovered here. As a result it has not been affected by mining, and did not grow in size. It remains a charming village in its fine rural surroundings, and one which is commemorated in the finest parish history written in Wales.

The old grammar school at Ysgeifiog

Remains of a stone cross in the churchyard at Ysgeifiog

Ysgeifiog

Ysgeifiog is a small village situated in the middle of pastoral countryside between the A55 and the A541 Denbigh-Mold road. It may be approached from Holywell, or via a minor road close to Nannerch.

It is an ancient settlement, the present church being on holy ground of long standing. The original stone church burnt down in 1837.

The area has yielded a number of prehistoric relics and burial mounds, one of the most significant being an artefact which was discovered in 1816. A farming family named Morris lived at Bryn Seion farm. In a field, fairly close to the farm, there stood a cairn of stones and near this was a kiln used by farmers for burning lime. One day the two Morris brothers were working at the kiln when they spotted an artefact which they thought was iron. When they returned to the farm in the evening they took it with them and threw it into a corner, in case they should ever have need of it. A few months went by, and one day some gypsies came to the farm collecting rags and old iron. One gypsy spotted the object and exclaimed to his companion 'See there! Tis gold!' On hearing this one of the brothers grabbed hold of it, and a struggle followed which was only cut short when the farm dog intervened and saw the gypsies off. The Morris' made it known that they had an item of antiquity value, and it was not long before the Marquis of Westminster heard of it. He offered £220 for it and this was accepted.

During the Medieval period traders would journey many miles across country on clearly defined routes, transporting their wares on their pack-ponies. They would travel in large groups, for taking a journey of any distance could be a dangerous undertaking; robbers and other law-breakers would frequently lie in wait for unsuspecting travellers. Ysgeifiog became an important resting point for traders, and one can well imagine what a bustling place it would have been. It was still an itinerants respite place in the seventeenth century, when stage-coaches would thunder into the village. (Northop was another stopping point.)

By the mid-eighteenth century much improved, and more direct, turnpike roads were constructed, and after 1772 it became possible to travel in greater comfort towards St Asaph and the coast, and Ysgeifiog was by-passed.

Walking around the village today you will see some buildings of interest. The Fox Inn dates from the eighteenth century, and welcomed many weary travellers in the past. Close to the church is the Old Rectory, which dates from 1780. The school was built in 1817 and in 1841 it was extended. It has an attractive feature in its bellcote.

There was a custom in Ysgeifiog that at a funeral of a member of their family the well-to-do would distribute small rolls of bread to the poor, who would come in large numbers to pay their last respects. Later small amounts of money were substituted. There was also a custom in the parish for a funeral procession to stop at every crossroads on the way to the church, in order to rehearse the Lord's Prayer.

William Edwards was born in Caerwys in 1790, but became known as 'Will Ysgeifiog'. He was a carpenter who had a natural talent as a poet, and was able to master the difficult strict metres. Much of his work appeared in periodicals and he won eisteddfod prizes. But he suffered from very severe bouts of depression, and his mental health gave rise to such concern that he was committed to an asylum more than once. On one occasion he escaped from the asylum, and went to the Crown Inn at Denbigh where he terrified the landlord and his wife by insisting that he was George III – who also happened to be insane – and demanding that they should round up all his troops. He is buried at Ysgeifiog.

One of the pioneers of Methodism in Flintshire was also born at Ysgeifiog. John Owen (1733-1776) was converted to the faith after hearing Daniel Rowland preaching at Llandyrnog. His farmhouse home, Y Berthen Gron, became a centre of worship in the area. Owen was the object of frequent persecution, especially in Holywell, and the then High Sheriff of Flintshire was anxious to put a stop to his activities. But despite this, the cause continued and gathered support. A chapel was built on land close to Y Berthen Gron in 1775, with almost the entire cost being borne by Owen himself. He rode all the way to Llangurig to ask Daniel Rowland if he would be prepared to deliver the first sermon, to which he agreed. Sadly, on his journey back to Ysgeifiog, Owen died suddenly.

Postscript

Three years ago a report was published which revealed that eighty per cent of British people live in urban areas. But a subsequent sample clearly suggested a dissatisfaction with town and city life, and nine-tenths of those interviewed longed for an entirely different lifestyle, within what they regarded as the idyllic environment of a village.

The reality of village life today is, of course, rather different. The move towards centralisation has hit the entity of the village community hard, and many of the traditional values of the small community are on the decline. Many village schools have been forced to close, there has been a drastic reduction of the rural public transport system, while the village shop is fighting for survival, its existence now threatened by the out-of-town supermarket.

But despite all this there is also a good deal of evidence that villages today are far from dead. Indeed there are those who are quite prepared to fight for the survival of their individual communities. A notable example in North Wales is Groes, near Denbigh. When the village shop and post office was threatened with closure, the villagers worked together in order to preserve their way of life. They called themselves Menter Ardal Groes *(Groes Local Initiative)*, and the result of all their efforts has been rewarded. They were so successful, in fact, that delegations from other European countries have visited Groes in order to learn something which will enable them to halt the decline of villages. Television film crews have also been attracted by this enterprise of ordinary people.

There is a lot happening in villages throughout Wales. Our nation is a land of small communities, and the community values which we regard as central to Welshness, are the values of the village.

Other titles about north-eastern Wales

THE LAND OF OLD RENOWN
– GEORGE BORROW IN WALES
Dewi Roberts; £4.50

A TOUR IN WALES by Thomas Pennant
An old classic abridged by David Kirk; £5.75

BOTH SIDES OF THE BORDER
An anthology on the Welsh Border Region
by Dewi Roberts; £4.75

Revd John Parker's TOUR OF WALES AND ITS CHURCHES
Abridged by Edgar W. Parry; £4.75

THE NORTH WALES PATH and 10 selected walks
Dave Salter and Dave Worrall; £4.50

CIRCULAR WALKS IN NORTH EASTERN WALES
Jim Grindle; £4.50

WALKS IN AND AROUND THE BERWYN MOUNTAINS
John Tranter; £4.50

HAUNTED CLWYD
Richard Holland; £3.50

SUPERNATURAL CLWYD
Richard Holland; £4.50

PLACE-NAMES OF DEE AND ALUN
Hywel Wyn Owen; £3.75

THE HISTORY OF THE RIVER DEE
Mike Griffiths; £7.95

For our full booklist and order forms please contact:
Gwasg Carreg Gwalch,
12 Iard yr Orsaf, Llanrwst, Dyffryn Conwy
☎ (01492) 642031